MY COUNTRY CHILDHOOD

A nostalgic roam through childhood memories of life in the countryside by some of our most influential writers, actors and journalists, selected from *Country Living* magazine's much-loved *Country Childhood* series. Share Laurie Lee's lyrical memories of childhood games and rituals in his Gloucestershire village; Joanna Lumley's passion for the rhythm and rules of the countryside, and John Nettles' love for the ubiquitous white clay and beautiful turquoise sea of his Cornish childhood home. Each of the fifty contributions captures an individual sense of time, place and personality, and together they provide a picture of country life across the British Isles.

MY COUNTRY CHILDHOOD

MY COUNTRY CHILDHOOD

Edited by

Susy Smith

Magna Large Print Books
Long Preston, North Yorkshire,
BD23 4ND, England.

920.02
LP

British Library Cataloguing in Publication Data.

Smith, Susy edited by
My country childhood.

A catalogue record of this book is
available from the British Library

ISBN   0-7505-1767-0

First published in Great Britain in 1999
by Hodder and Stoughton
A division of Hodder Headline PLC

Published in Large Print 2001 by arrangement with
Hodder & Stoughton Ltd.

Magna Large Print is an imprint of Library Magna Books Ltd.
Printed and bound in Great Britain by
T.J. (International) Ltd., Cornwall, PL28 8RW

ACKNOWLEDGEMENTS

Maeve Binchy reprinted by kind permission of the author and the author's agent, Christine Green. *Libby Purves* reprinted by kind permission of the author and the author's agent, Lisa Eveleigh. *Rosamunde Pilcher* reprinted by kind permission of the author and the author's agent, Felicity Bryan. *Laurie Lee* reprinted by kind permission of Peters, Fraser and Dunlop Group Ltd. *Nigel Slater* reprinted by kind permission of the author and the author's agent, Lucas Alexander Whitley. *Joanna Trollope* reprinted by kind permission of the author and the author's agent, Peters, Fraser and Dunlop Group Ltd.

CONTENTS

LETTER FROM THE EDITOR

A childhood spent in the countryside leaves memories to treasure for ever. For many of us in the British Isles, these memories are sharply defined by the rhythms of the season – bluebells in spring, strawberries in summer, blackberries in autumn and the red berries of the holly bush in winter. Then there are the special games that we associate with particular times of year – hunting for frogspawn, collecting chestnuts to polish into conkers, or praying for the village pond to freeze over for skating.

There is a sense of adventure about growing up in the countryside – a seemingly endless landscape full of secret walks and hiding places, where we can escape from the rules of the adult world and, maybe, spend a night out under the stars. We always remember the days when nature took the upper hand – when heavy snowfall kept us away from schools or those summers when the sun never stopped shining and we picnicked in the scorched fields day after day.

But there is more to a country childhood than the memories – this is a time when we discover the richness of the natural world and delight in learning the names of plants, animals and birds. Lessons learnt in the countryside are never forgotten.

Over the last fourteen years, *Country Living Magazine's* much loved *Country Childhood* series has celebrated the power of these memories. Reading through this unique collection provides a fascinating insight into the life and personality of each writer, and will no doubt stir memories of your own. 'I would love to have it all over again,' writes author Richard Adams, 'to lean from my bedroom window on an early summer night: to watch the great orange moon rise slowly behind the oak trees on the left, gaining to brilliant silver as it rose high to illuminate the moth-filled garden, the great cornfield beyond the further hedge and the bluebell woods plainly visible on the clear horizon four miles away.' I'm sure anyone who grew up in the countryside would agree.

Happy reading!

Susy Smith

RICHARD ADAMS

I was born in 1920, the fourth child of a country doctor, who was 50 years old at that time. My mother was 36. She had been a nurse at Bath and had married my father after meeting him at Martock in Somerset, where she had been sent from the hospital as resident nurse to a patient of his. After their marriage they moved to Newbury.

In 1916 my father bought a beautiful house at Wash Common, which was then a village on the southern side of Newbury, high above the Kennet Valley. There were three acres of half-wild garden, and it is this flowering wilderness that constitutes my first childhood memories. Part of the garden was formal – a big lawn that included a tennis court, a putting green and a small croquet ground, together with a herbaceous border and groups of flowerbeds tended by Thorn, the gardener.

I was rather a solitary child, for my sister was nine years older than I and my brother seven. There had been a third child, Robert, who had died, aged two, in the terrible flu epidemic that decimated Europe in 1919, the year after the Great War ended. I was mostly left to myself, to play among the shrubberies, the meadows and copses which made up the whole small estate. I had imaginary friends who joined in my games and adventures, and had their own 'houses', in which we would spend time together, plotting our imaginary enterprises. My principal imaginary friend was called Stonepath. His house lay in the heart of a great clump of gold azaleas, the scent of which, in June, drifted across the whole garden. By contrast, Photel's house was at the top of a big Spanish chestnut tree. This tree had been pollarded, so that there was a flat place on which you could sit, with lateral boughs growing upwards all around you to form a kind of cave of branches. Decité's house was a natural cavity at the heart of a big clump of rhododendrons. The thick clump was entirely waterproof and I used to enjoy going round to Decité's house when it was raining. You felt you had outwitted the rain, so to speak.

Newbury lies on the River Kennet. On the north side of the Vale of Kennet lie the

White Horse Downs, while on the south side lie the Downs that extend from Basingstoke to Winchester and include Watership Down in their length. My father used to take me to walk with him beside the Kennet and show me the trout rising to the evening fly. He himself sometimes used to cast a fly, and he had several friends who did so. When I was about fourteen, he began teaching me how to fish myself. The pleasure lay less in actually catching fish than in the peace to be found beside a fairly big river like the Kennet, where in those days a silent fisherman might expect to see all manner of wildlife, including otters, badgers and herons.

The Downs were an entirely different kind of country. Being made of chalk, they possessed their own grasses, herbs and birds. In those days, the Downs were not ploughed but were kept for grazing sheep. My father knew, as patients, several of the shepherds on the Downs and we used to stop and chat to them in the course of our walks. I learned to know the characteristic wildflowers and the birds – the yellow-hammer and linnet; and the silverweed, salad burnet and wild orchids.

Our house stood on a kind of plateau

south of Newbury, with the Kennet to the north. On the other side of the plateau, going towards Andover, is the county boundary between Berkshire and Hampshire – the little Enborne brook. Here my father took me to paddle for the first time. To call it paddling is an understatement, for it was quite a thrilling adventure for a little boy. I put on rubber sandshoes and stripped to a pair of bathing drawers. Then I got into the water and began wading downstream, while my father, on the bank, pretended to be taking no notice. The water grew deeper and deeper until it was well up to my navel and a bit over. I had not gone more than a few yards before I found brickwork under my feet and the stream curved to the left among the ruins of an old mill. At the far end, the stream went over a little ford into a deep pool, so here the adventure ended, among the meadowsweet and the hovering dragonflies of midsummer.

It is difficult for people nowadays to imagine what things were like before motor cars became common and roads were tarred. The dusty roads of my infancy were intended for the hooves of horses, and of sheep and cattle driven to market. About 200 yards from our house lay the village pond, and here we would often see a herd of cows being kept knee-deep in the water by the dogs, while their masters, who might have driven them seven or eight miles already, went into The Bell or The Gun – our locals – for a well-earned pint. Then they would drive them down Wash Hill to Newbury market, the cattle lowing, 'flopping' all over the road and raising a dust which lay white on the hedges and had its own peculiar and rather pleasant smell – one of the smells of summer, like mown hay and clumps of stinging nettles. The sheep did not go to the pond. They went by in a pattering of little hooves, a continual jostling and baa'ing and barking of dogs.

My father was doctor to the Newbury racecourse, and as soon as I was old enough I used to join the rest of the family at the race meetings. My chin on the rails of the paddock, I would watch the beautiful, sleek horses led slowly round and round, while their owners and trainers chatted in the middle, with overcoated jockeys.

We never went away anywhere, and I suppose to a lot of children nowadays my childhood might seem rather a restricted one, bound as it was by much solitude, by a few friends of my own age and by the warm companionship of my parents. Yet I cannot regret a minute of it and would love to have it all over again – to lean from my bedroom window on an early summer night; to watch the great orange moon rise slowly behind the oak trees on the left, gaining to brilliant silver as it rose high to illuminate the moth-filled garden, the great cornfield beyond the further hedge and the bluebell woods through which, many years later, Hazel, Bigwig, Fever and the rest were to make their long journey to Watership Down, plainly visible on the clear horizon four miles away.

NINA BAWDEN

Really, it was my mother who was the country child. Married to a marine engineer and living in a small house near the London docks, she saw the suburban landscape around her as a dreary waste and pined for the Norfolk of her childhood: the heaths, the woodland, the wide skies. Her nostalgia for a vanished Eden infected me when I was very small and by 1939, when I was thirteen and about to be evacuated from London with my school, I was entranced by the whole concept of 'living in the country' and expected Paradise.

Oddly, perhaps, I was not disappointed (I suppose I should call it my adolescence, but thirteen-year-old girls were still children then) and remember perfect happiness. My mother and my brothers had left London for the Welsh border country and, although my school was evacuated to a mining town where I had to stay with foster parents in term time, my real life (in imagination when it could not be in fact) was lived with my family, in one enormous room of an old farmhouse in a beautiful valley between Montgomery and Bishop's Castle.

The life we lived there, without electricity or telephone or running water, was probably closer to my mother's childhood memories of country life than it might have been had she chosen to find safety from the Blitz in the Home Counties. We fetched our water from the pump in the yard until the well ran dry, at which point we took the trap and a milk churn to the brook. We had one hanging oil lamp and two Tilley lamps, and candles. My mother cooked (amazingly well, I realise now) on a small tin oven on an oil stove, or on the hob of the fire. The lavatory was a privy at the end of the vegetable garden, a three-seater with a large hole, a medium-size hole and a small hole. (I hated to be seen visiting there and have been constipated all my life as a result.) We had an old battery wireless to which my mother listened, but the batteries were always running down and so the news of bombing and battles came to us very ghostly and faint, as if being transmitted from another world a long way away.

I listened with my mother sometimes but the world of the farm absorbed me to the exclusion of everything else, even concern for my father who was on convoy duty in the North Sea. Collecting eggs, shutting up the chickens that roamed free all day in the orchard, helping with the harvest – these were expected pleasures. But I was a convert to country living and, like all converts, extra zealous. I begged to be given a fork and a pile of manure, to be allowed to muck out the cowsheds and the pig sties. Cleaning out the privy was the pinnacle of my achievement in this area, though I must admit that I was paid for it: the farmer, unable to credit that a 'townie' would take up his offer, had mentioned the huge sum of five pounds. But he paid me punctiliously and took me more seriously afterwards, teaching me to drive a horse and harrow, to dip sheep and, one wonderful cold winter's night, got me out of bed to hold the lamp at a difficult birth. His arm was buried up to his shoulder inside the cow; he sweated and grunted as she threw him from side to side. He pulled until the tiny front hooves appeared, held firm in his hand, and the calf was born with a slippery rush of mucus and blood. I said, when it had risen to its tottery feet, 'This is the best moment of my whole life.' And instead of laughing, as I feared he would, my farmer friend said, 'I never get tired of it; it always gets me in the throat.'

Very few farmers had cars. We took the pony and trap if we went shopping in the town. I and my brothers walked miles: gathering blackberries, climbing the Long Mynd to collect the little low-growing black wineberries, and picking nuts from the hedgerows for our red squirrel, Henry, who lived with us for one short enchanted year. I did the post round while our postman got his harvest in, riding up into the hills where most people still spoke Welsh but managed a few English words for the London girl on her borrowed black pony. I knew A.E. Housman by heart and shouted my favourite poems out load as I trotted through the valleys of Onny and Teme and Clun, taking his love for those quiet towns and rivers into my heart and my life for ever.

MAEVE BINCHY

I have a very firm earliest memory. I, the first-born, was three and a half and my mother was expecting another child. I was constantly asking God to send me a new brother or sister so I was outraged when the baby arrived because all the attention shifted from me to this small red-faced thing in a cot. I had been praying for this moment; and now here was this 'thing', wailing and wailing, and everybody was saying how beautiful it was. 'Honestly,' I said, 'I would have preferred a rabbit!' I had wanted a rabbit for ages, and for the next three years I wanted to send my sister back. When I think of the great friendship I have with her now I cringe at the thought of it.

Home was initially in Dun Laoghaire and later in Dalkey, Co. Dublin. I love Dalkey. It's not just a sentimental attachment – I just love the hills and the sea and walking over Dalkey Hill, along the Green Road in Killiney and down the Vico Road. Of course, I got very used to walking as a child. I was the eldest of four so there was always somebody in a pram – never, alas, a rabbit – to be wheeled out for a walk.

At the age of five I went to St Anne's, a lovely little nursery school in Clarinda Park in Dun Laoghaire. It was run by a Mrs Russell, who was one of those wonderful old women with white hair and a straight back that you always saw as somebody's grandmother in old films. There were two other ladies, her nieces, I think, both called Miss Bath. One was fat and one was thin: with typical childish cruelty we called them 'Hot Bath' and 'Cold Bath'. We didn't have a school uniform, but my great excitement was wearing a big bow on my head. The bow was ironed for me every morning and I went off to school looking like a little cockatoo!

My next school was a convent school in Killiney, Co. Dublin, run by the Order of the Holy Child Jesus. These nuns had come to Ireland after the war; they were terribly nice, but they didn't understand the Irish language or its pronunciation, nor its importance in the school curriculum. Consequently the first year that the Leaving Certificate examination was taken in that school, I think nearly every student failed Irish.

All my school reports said that I was bright but lazy: I didn't stir myself enough. However, in those days being at the top of the class wasn't nearly as important as being good at games. To have big strong arms and be able to hit the hockey ball miles down the pitch – that was real status. I didn't enjoy games. We all wore green uniforms tied in the middle and we looked like potato sacks of various sizes. I remember standing on the hockey pitch, my legs blue with the cold, hoping that all the action would remain at the far end and that I would not be called on to do anything.

But I enjoyed netball. I was very tall, which led the games mistress to believe that I had potential on the netball team as a shooter. I was a great success. I was in the First Eleven team for two whole years, which was lovely because we went out to other convents on Wednesday afternoons to play netball, and we had tea and buns afterwards. I was, to use modern parlance, a lethal striker.

Apart from hockey, the other thing I hated – we all hated it – was being dragged to the beach by the nuns. They would say: 'Come on girls, show some school spirit.' It was easy for them to say that when they had about 9,000 black petticoats on them and they didn't have to go into the icy sea and show school spirit.

I wanted to be a saint. This was not just a childhood ambition: I wanted to be a saint until I was about 22. It wasn't a question of 'I hope it will happen to me'; I was quite convinced that I would be a saint.

I had a very special relationship with God. I regarded him as a friend, and Irish, and somebody who knew me well. He had sent particular tortures my way – like not being good at games (until the marvellous netball 'discovery'), and being fat at school.

I worried a lot about people who didn't keep up their own religion. I had a friend whose father was a Protestant – a lovely man whom we all adored because he used to give us fourpenny ice-creams when every other father only gave us twopenny ones. He used to drive his wife and children to Mass and then go for a walk on Dun Laoghaire pier. I would spend hours with his daughter, wondering if I would be damned and roasted in hell. I felt that if he wasn't converted to Catholicism he should at least be going to his own church. Imagine this poor unfortunate man being harangued by his eight-year-old daughter and her friend saying, 'Have you thought about it – the devil and the pain that goes on for ever?' The more I look back on it, the more I realise what a poisonous little person I was – and having an over-developed imagination didn't help.

My mother was terrific at explaining the facts of life to us. She told me that she never had them explained to her, so she was determined that she was going to explain them clearly to us. I had known from a very early age how children were born because we had rabbits in a hutch (finally), so there was no great mystery about birth; but I wanted to know how babies were conceived. She told me and I decided that this was absolutely impossible; wasn't it terribly sad that my mother was going mad? She was in bed with flu when I discussed the subject with my father.

'I'm very sorry to tell you, Daddy, that Mummy is going insane,' I said.

'Why?' he enquired.

'I couldn't tell you the things she said,' I replied tactfully, 'but she has a very peculiar idea of how children are conceived.' I gave him a broad outline of her description. 'Don't you think we should get her to a doctor?' I asked with great concern.

'Ah, no,' he said. 'I think she had a point.'

I thought to myself, 'Isn't Daddy an amazingly loyal man!'

I think I was extraordinarily lucky to be born into a family about whom I have nothing but good memories. I was lonely sometimes, I suppose – feeling that I would not be successful because I was fat, for example – but that was only outside home; at home I never felt fat. At home I felt very loved and very special. My sisters, my brother and I have all remained extremely friendly and when we talk and think back on our childhood, we do so with laughter and affection, not with any sense of fear or dread. We simply think how lucky we were.

PETER BOWLES

Although I was born in London, it wasn't long before my family moved to a small thatched cottage in Upper Boddington, Northamptonshire. To me, as a small boy, the most distinguishing feature of our new home was the enormous inglenook fireplace, but a later visit revealed that, like so many things in childhood, it actually wasn't that big at all. Days spent here meant simple living with a garden full of potatoes, carrots, spinach and onions, and peas so sweet that we ate them in their pods. Complete with a small lawn and walnut tree, that fenced garden was also a happy home to our family dog and talking jackdaw.

The cottage belonged to the local manor house where my father worked as, among other things, a chauffeur and butler. But I was never intimidated by Boddington Manor, an Elizabethan house so much bigger than our own. Perhaps this is because it was wartime and there were refugees staying there, providing me with a constant stream of playmates. Indeed, I can remember the prisoners of war being driven through the village on the backs of lorries, always waving.

I strayed wherever I chose in the summer, tobogganed down gentle hills in the winter and rode my tricycle all year round – until I fell off. The scar on my forehead is still visible. I remember lying on the kitchen table staring at a swinging oil lamp while being stitched up by the local doctor.

When I think back to my early childhood, the fragrance of apples fills my mind, for I adored the manor's apple house and can still envisage apple after apple being wrapped in newspaper for storage. Even at three years old, I'd wander near it, whistling away in the hope of being 'discovered' as the next whistling radio star. I think I must always have been a show-off for I have a vague memory of joining the local ladies in their pantomine at the village hall. Apparently, it was quite a job to get me off the stage.

The old village school, with its one teacher and one class of children up to seven years old, almost certainly assisted my career. From as young as three, I'd walk down the lanes to get there. Within a few years, I was reading Dickens and so, when I moved to

Nottingham at six years old, I was inevitably asked to read to the rest of the class time and time again.

After school one day I found about a hundred eggs on a nearby farm and threw them at a tin balanced on a wall. It was the only time I can remember my father being cross with me. It was the same farm where my father would choose a duck or chicken for Christmas and wring its neck himself. This was the way all the farmers lived: even when I was four years old, I wasn't shocked at the sight of a pig being killed and then hung up by its hind legs and slit down the middle.

Throughout my childhood, summers were spent in an Eighteenth-Century stone house in Wigtownshire, Scotland, where my grandfather worked for the factor, or estate manager. It was a remote place and I can vividly remember my alarm at being woken one morning by an enormous crash – a stag had trapped its antlers in one of the windows. The area had an overwhelming smell of bracken, and the hundreds of huge prickly pine trees seemed to beckon me to climb them. But it was my active imagination that led to some serious frights: once I convinced myself that a whole pack of wolves was waiting for me at the foot of a tree, and I used to drive my parents nuts when I woke them at 5am to feed my imaginary horse.

My father, grandfather and I would go for long walks, armed with carved sticks to ward off the adders. It was a joy to ramble with them, owing to their incredible knowledge of wildlife. They could name every butterfly, tree and flower. Even the birds' eggs in the hedgerows – which I used to take to blow – were identified. I never seemed to pick up this skill, which I later discovered was due to me being colour blind.

My other grandfather – who was born in 1864 and was one of the last horse coach drivers in the country – lived on the open land outside Huntingdon. He kept a pig of whom I was very fond, and a horse that he brushed tirelessly while making friendly horse noises. But I remember most distinctly the daily wartime sight of my grandfather putting on a suit to listen to the six o'clock news. The funny thing was that he didn't own a radio. He would place a glass against the wall to listen in on next door's, and relay to us everything that was happening beyond the peaceful countryside.

AMANDA BURTON

The memories of my idyllic childhood just outside Derry, Northern Ireland seem to be in glorious Technicolor. Home was a bustling Nineteenth-Century house with rounded windows and a large porthole in which I would curl up to read at night. The house stood next to the local primary school, where my father was headmaster, and it had marvellous views of Ballougry, an area with too few dwellings even to be called a village.

I was the youngest of four daughters in a domesticated family, and I remember the kitchen as the core of our home. Potatoes, beans, peas and beetroot were always cooked fresh from the garden – a passion of my father's, whose pupils also had vegetable plots. His shadow, complete with garden tools, would walk past the window at all hours. The weeding, however, he loathed and there was bribery involved in persuading us to take that chore off his hands. Packed with peonies, daisy lawns and

Californian poppies, our walled garden stretched the length of the school grounds. A small gate led to the added luxury of the playing fields – ideal for summer games of rounders and tennis. It is these gardens with their surrounding fields and quarries that I remember most.

For hours I used to go off on my bicycle with a sense of freedom that seems astounding in retrospect. There was a stream at the bottom of the nearby valley, where we used to collect sticklebacks and tadpoles and snatch glimpses of the odd trout that we could never catch. Walks made daily outings, particularly to the local fort, which I believe inspired the hymn, 'There is a Green Hill Far Away'. We'd wander more than a mile to The Border Store, a traditional Irish shop made of old corrugated iron, which sold everything from coal to tins of sweets. I knew the land like the back of my hand, hiding sweets in the nooks and crannies of ancient walls, never doubting that I'd find them later.

The contrasting seasons had a tremendous influence on me. Harsh, stormy winters often lasted from September to April and I can still see my father digging into mounds of snow surrounding the house. Then, in springtime, domestic tasks came to the fore. As soon as it became warmer, the week-long ritual of washing all the blankets in the bath and laying the rugs out on the lawn to be beaten began.

Summer, with its short nights, was the height of activity in the area's farming community. But because of my father's job, we could spend our days as a family. My mother would wake everyone early, we'd pick up provisions and gather twigs ready for fabulous Ulster fry-ups cooked on an open fire. These family picnics took place in the most beautiful spots, with lakes that had ten islands stretching through them. Sometimes, when we got home, we'd find a trout sticking out of the letter box as a gift from an appreciative pupil – a glistening thank you card!

For holidays, we would rent a house in the deep south of Ireland or drive across the border to Donegal. We rarely spent time in cities, except for the annual Dublin Horse Show, where we'd take endless photographs of people in red coats on black stallions – every one the same. I adored Donegal with its isolated beaches and enormous ocean, which you knew stretched as far as America.

My first memory is of sitting in the mouth of a cave at four years old, watching my family swim.

As the nights drew in, we felt we could get up to all sorts of mischief – especially on Hallowe'en. It was the one night we'd be allowed to run around on the road and get up to no good, although we never really did. Before the Troubles began and fireworks were banned, I'd get so excited that I'd start them off a week before time.

When the daily chore of travelling to high school in the city began, I was devastated. I adored my home and was deeply in love with my parents. I hated being parted from them: on Girl Guide camp when I was ten, I climbed on to a rock to see the lights of Derry in the distance – shattered at the thought of them being so far away.

When I began to understand the spiritual side of Ireland, my surroundings seemed increasingly romantic. I was fifteen when I discovered Irish music. My sister and I would spend our evenings going to Galway pubs to see bands such as The Chieftains, begging for lifts in and out of town as the last train left before 6pm.

Despite my love for Ireland, I left to study

drama in Manchester at eighteen. Ireland remains a huge part of me, but I have a great fondness for England, too – Derbyshire is my greatest love, thanks to the Central Television series, *Peak Practice*. But working in Belfast last year, I was so excited about returning to my roots. The places I revisited still had a unique magic.

BARBARA CASTLE

I was brought up in the industrial North – always in or near a mining or manufacturing area where people earned their living amid grime and soot. My father was an Inspector of Taxes, so was moved around regularly. I was born in Chesterfield, the heart of a mining community. My early years were passed in Pontefract, where life was coloured by the surrounding pits. Then we moved to Bradford, whose majestic stone buildings were blackened by smoke from its woollen mills. Yet I always considered myself a country girl.

There are two reasons for this. The first is that in the 1920's, when I was growing up (I was born in 1910), there was still evidence everywhere that industry had been imposed on an essentially rustic way of life. Though traumatic in its impact, industrialisation did not run deep. Pontefract, for instance, was by instinct and origin a market town. When I revisited it recently I found that the street names of its modest centre still reflect its agricultural roots: Buttercross, Cornmarket, Ropergate, Beastfair. The market gardens were still in the town centre, where as a child I had been taken by my mother to buy the one penny liquorice roots that had given birth to the town's famous liquorice works. Liquorice allsorts and Pontefract cakes are still my favourite confections – far superior to chocolate in my view.

I discovered the same rural roots in industrial Lancashire when I became MP for Blackburn in 1945. An old party stalwart presented me with a 'Lankisher dictionary', from which I learnt how to interpret mysterious words like 'winter hedge'. This, I gathered, was a clothes horse, and the phrase betrays the cotton textile industry's origins as a domestic industry in the sur-rounding villages. In summer the women would dry their washing on the garden hedge; in winter they had to put it by the fire indoors on a 'winter hedge'.

The second reason why I always considered myself a country girl was my family. We were Socialists, which meant that we believed that the beauties of Britain's countryside belonged to all of us. In those early days politics was very much concerned with the right of town-bound people to have access to the mountains and other joys of the open spaces, which they claimed as their heritage. So there were the Clarion cycling clubs, the Ramblers' Association and the campaigns to establish national parks and create long-distance walking routes like the Pennine Way. We wanted those who slaved in the mills to be free to escape to the open air above the polluted industrial towns.

My mother was what I describe in my autobiography as a 'William Morris Socialist'. Like Morris she sought to create beauty amid the industrial ugliness and keep the spirit of pastoral England alive. Our modest little home in Love Lane, Pontefract was sited next to a row of miners' cottages, separated from us by a cinder track. She was not dismayed by the unpropitious surroundings in which she found herself. Every May Day she sent myself, my brother and sister out into the nearby fields to pick any wildflowers we could find to decorate the maypole she erected on the patch of dusty unkempt grass we called a garden. I was about three or four years old at the time. I can still remember clutching a long piece of ribbon as we romped round the maypole with our friends from the miners' homes, who, I suspect, believed we were slightly mad.

Later the family moved to a leafy suburb of Pontefract. I thought it was paradise. The 1914-18 War and the subsequent slump had sterilised the development of Carlton Park Avenue. Our house abutted on to a stretch of half-cultivated allotments in which my brother and I played cowboys and Indians with a gang of noisy friends. I used to flatten myself among the cabbages to avoid discovery, my face pressed against the friendly earth. The avenue also boasted a large stretch of grass opposite our house on to which my father would occasionally emerge from his study (he was a bookish man) to teach us cricket. This would consist of his hurling hard cricket balls at us, for us to catch. When I muffed my catch, hurting my fingers, he would bawl at me: 'Cup your hands!'

But it was in smoke-blackened Bradford, to which we moved in 1920, that I first came into contact with nature at its most bleak: the Yorkshire moors. Initially, I wept when I learnt that we were to leave Pontefract for this metropolis, passionately telling my mother: 'I will never become a town girl.' Yet it wasn't long before I found that even Bradford, a large industrial city where workers from the villages had been crowded into factories at an early stage, was not very far removed from its country roots. A tram ride from the city centre would take me up the hillside and into some of Britain's wildest countryside. I loved scrambling over the rough grass and the stone walls of those windy heights, savouring the solitude. 'Wuthering Heights' became my spiritual home.

Since then I have become a Southerner, marrying a Berkshire man, entering Parliament and living in London until recently.

The great bond in our marriage was our love of the countryside. There was plenty of friendly bickering between us about the merits of our respective backgrounds. Ted was a Downsman whose father came from Wantage. I was a product of the moors, proclaiming their superiority over the softer versions of the South. But in fact I came to love the Downs as well, and Ted and I walked many a mile along the Ridgeway, back-packing our way from village to village during a long weekend. Later we helped Tom Stephenson of the Ramblers' Association to forge the Pennine Way. Today I live amid the rural delights of the Chiltern hills.

So, for all my long years in London, I never became a town girl.

FRANK DELANEY

All my life has been enriched by countryside. It is where I grew up; it is where I now live. The one, over 50 years ago, Tipperary, green, lush, still and ripe; the other, today, Somerset, green, lush, still and ripe.

My first remembered awareness of what I now think of as great privilege came in the June of my fifth year. 'Ne'er cast a clout 'til May is out' had ever been misinterpreted by my mother as meaning the month of May, when it actually refers to the may or hawthorn blossom. So in June we took off our shoes and went barefoot in the grasses of the big fields that, like a wide ocean, surrounded our house.

The blades of grass poked cool spears between my toes and in the stream the mud squeezed softly over my instep. Every time I smell wild garlic now – and the Somerset lanes fill up with it – I see that brown ooze on my white, bare foot. (The wild garlic also evokes a passionate love affair but that is another story.)

I remember most the light: looking out from the inside into bright sun and blue mountains; or looking from outside into farmyard sheds, a blacksmith's forge, cows at milking time. I can still feel the contrasts of warmth on my shoulders and cool on my face, standing at a farmhouse door watching the women inside washing blankets in high summer. I still smell the dust from the hay in the high barns.

Most reminiscences of country childhood dwell mainly on the flavour of summer. Always longer, always warmer, always gold. Good memories make their events longer than they were; bad memories seem shorter, sharper, no matter how long the occasion lasted. That is probably why we all reach for summer first.

Not me. When I think of the countryside I grew up in, it falls into memories of the seasons. Now I divide my life in Somerset into the same four enjoyments. It always begins with autumn. An old farming theory holds that we most love the time of year into which we were born. I was born in October and I am happiest in autumn, in the days that have a flavour and a smell, when everything has mellowed.

The most significant events of my life have happened in autumn. And time has led me to believe that they have all been good things (the law of averages has no influence over memory). Those dark blue evening skies when the sun has set, the boxes of apples from the garden, the marvelling at how often the lawns still need cutting, and the smell of woodsmoke when there is no woodsmoke – that is my present autumn.

My past autumns included finding the thickest clusters of hazelnuts hidden under bunched leaves; watching for the day a tree turned colour to see whether one could actually see the leaves go from green to brown; and then, as the leaves fell, finding the husk of the bird's nest that had proven so elusive in May.

This makes it sound as if no other seasons

existed. Unfair to the brilliance of the frost that came thick as light snow in December. Unfair to the thick, thick rain of January and the first moment in February when the evenings stretched – just a little but noticeably. Unfair to what the Irish poet Kavanagh called 'the tremendous silence of mid-July', in which everything may happen and nothing does.

I have kept the best of my country living until last – the aspect that has haunted me for as long as I can recall, which still plays a part in every day, and which probably, if I examine it, proved a serious reason for moving from London to be in the country again. We're talking weather. Not any hour of any day goes by, it seems to me, in which I do not make some observation to myself of weather. I am fascinated by where the wind is coming from, when it turns, how long it stays in the east, whether when it turns south-west it will bring rain. There is a wonderful moment that happens in late June, earlier if we're lucky, when an African wind arrives.

I love to see the rain coming, to see showers in the distance. Up our lane, there is a small, high plateau and from there I can see the distance of Somerset, off out beyond

Glastonbury Tor, out, it seems from the cloud formations, to the sea at Weston or Minehead. One day I counted five different showers out in those vistas, and if I still held the childhood belief that Jacob's Ladders are the means by which we climb to heaven I should have been able to go there many, many times.

ADAM FAITH

I was a kid and it was towards the end of the War. We were evacuated. Dumped on the back of a lorry under tarpaulin and driven out into the country one night from Acton, which had been bombed to death. We woke up the next morning near Newark in Nottinghamshire. It was a bit like falling through the twilight zone, really. I have a very clear memory of that moment. It was the first time I had ever experienced the country. I remember coming out of the cottage in the morning and seeing a big tree with blossom on it. I had never seen a tree that belonged to us before. Trees always belonged to streets and parks and other people's places. There was a field with cows in it. It was the first time I had ever seen cows. I thought I'd died and gone to heaven.

There was a kind of cleanliness in the country. It didn't smell of smoke, or bombs, or war. There were no violent noises. We were used to hearing people screaming, running, panic. It was another world. It wasn't as if we'd grown up watching programmes about it on the television thinking, 'Oh weird, that's the countryside.' We didn't know what the country was. No one had ever described it to us because no one had ever been near it. I hadn't even seen it in a book.

It was a friend of my uncle's who owned the cottage. It was thatched – a typical Ealing comedy or Miss Marple cottage: white, with black timbers. I don't remember a single thing about the inside. All my memories are to do with being outside: taking a jug out to the man in the pony-and-trap with his milk churns; going off on adventures with a bottle of orangeade tied on to my belt. We went off discovering, exploring, all the time.

After the War, when we were back living in Acton again, our old lady decided she wanted to live in a house, not a flat. We were given a brand new one in South Ruislip. It was only six miles from London, but in those days it may as well have been in the middle of Scotland. We used to spend all our time playing in the fields on the local farm, jumping the river (it was a stream really, but it felt like a river). Every day we traipsed back home dripping wet because, of course, we always fell in. When the stream iced up, we used to skate along it in our shoes.

The first sign that winter was round the corner was playing conkers. I remember baking them in the oven, putting them in vinegar, doing everything I possibly could to make them hard. I remember constantly sore knuckles.

I loved Ruislip, and when my mum decided she was fed up with it a couple of years later I didn't want to move back to the city. My mum hated the open spaces, the quiet. She was more at home walking on roads and pavements than through fields. If she'd been excited about the country, of course, we'd never have left it. We might even have moved further into it, and lived the proper rural life. We might never have come back from Newark. One of the most miserable days of my life was the day we got back to Acton. I remember walking up the high street in total abject misery. What did Acton have to offer after Ruislip?

When I got into show business almost the first thing I wanted to do was to find a place in the country again. Eventually I did move out – we bought a farm – and I've never really looked back. Being there is like taking Valium. It calms you. I don't feel I ever *live* in London, when I'm there. I *exist* in London; I *live* in the countryside. The ideal retirement for me will be sitting in a deck chair, in my garden, in the country. With our house in Ruislip there was a little garden, which seemed enormous to me when we first went there. I had my own vegetable patch and grew tomatoes and runner beans, and a cucumber plant with a little hat of glass over it. My brother started me off on it. I wanted to grow something. There's an incredible sense of achievement when things start to grow.

I've hankered after a vegetable garden ever since. At my house in the country, there's a courtyard garden enclosed by hawthorn bushes with a little gateway into it, and I was just thinking the other day that I could turn it into a vegetable garden, put a little hut in there, and sit there reading while my garden grows around me. I thought, 'It'll be just like my dad and his allotment in Acton.' Not that he ever kept it up really; he was never a gardener. But it was the thing to do, to have a bit of an allotment to try to grow some vegetables. Why did I never help him, when we moved back? Too busy chasing girls, I suppose.

PENELOPE FITZGERALD

When my father was demobilised from the army in 1919 he had no job to go to and nowhere to live. He was supporting his wife and two small children by writing a poem every week for *Punch*. Before the war he had taken the lease (or so he thought) of a small house looking on to Hampstead Heath, in London. But now it turned out that the writer Katherine Mansfield was living in it, and although she disliked the place it seems to have been impossible to ask her to leave. So, when I was two years old, we went to live in Balcombe, in East Sussex.

That meant I had my own room, looking out over a lawn with a cherry tree, splendid with white blossom in spring, and splendid, too, in the cherry season – but then the birds more or less lived in it, and I can't think there was ever much fruit left for us. With the walnut tree we did better. Mrs Ticehurst, who came in once a week to help out, knew the best (she said the only) recipe for walnut ketchup. Unfortunately, it was unaffordable: a hundred very young green walnuts, half a pint of best port wine, anchovies, brandy, horseradish, nutmegs, wine vinegar. Mrs Ticehurst herself admitted she had never made it. She pickled the walnuts, and so did we.

The garden was small, I suppose, for the country. I have been back to look at it since, but only once. I prefer to think of it as it was then, when I knew it was enormous. A large garden is one that a tame rabbit can get lost in, and my brother's rabbit was lost most of the time. I, too, had my hiding place. This was between the bushes of a double rose hedge which ran along one side of the lawn. They must, I think, have been *Rosa galica*; they certainly grew too tall for a tidy-looking hedge. Where I used to sit, beneath the level of the crowded leaves and the pink flowers, the ground was never quite dry, and the light fell only in patches. You could sit in a patch of sunlight and move along with it gradually as it shifted.

After a while I would be called back into the house to help. I couldn't be of help, but someone stood me on a chair at the kitchen table to see what was going on. I remember the business of 'going through' the raisins, bought from the grocer's by the shovelful: you had to sort out the small pieces of gravel. How did they get there in the first place? The rice, too, had to be 'picked over'. There were so many long, slow processes, but I knew (because I had heard people say so) that we were lucky to be living in modern, labour-saving times. We had no refrigerator and no telephone, but we had a clothes-washer, worked by turning a handle, and coloured tablecloths (that needed no bleaching) and stainless steel knives (that needed no cleaning). And however much there was to do there was a time, on hot summer afternoons, when everything seemed to run down almost to a stopping-point. The garden was silent, not a murmur even from the hens in their run behind the rose hedge; and inside the house the only sound, apart from the kitchen clock, was the redcurrant juice dripping slowly through the strainer into the jelly pan.

We walked long distances, my mother and I,

and so did most of Balcombe's inhabitants. Often we were delivering messages, or returning borrowed objects, or telling the baker and the grocer, who delivered three times a week, that what they had sent was not quite what had been asked for. On the way there and back, across the fields and by the roadside, I had my collecting to do. Feathers, pheasant feathers in particular, were needed for Red Indian headdresses. My brother, when he was at home, was a warrior brave and I was Minnehaha. Then there were horseshoe nails, cast horseshoes, snail shells, beechmast, pignuts, flints and wayside flowers. When I got home, everything was laid out on my bedroom window-sill to be counted and recounted, one of the most reassuring activities of all for a small child. Cataloguing easily becomes poetry. My mother read to me from Walter de la Mare's' *Peacock Pie* about the poor widow who planted her garden with weeds:

And now all summer she sits and sews
Where willow-herb, comfrey and bugloss blows,
Teasel and tansy, meadowsweet,
Campion, toadflax, and rough hawksbit;
Brown-bee orchis, and Peals of Bells;
Clover, burnet, and thyme she smells...

The naming of names, as de la Mare very well understood, is halfway to having magical power over things.

From time to time Lady Denman, the most important benefactress in the neighbourhood, took me out for what was then called a joy-ride in her chauffeur-driven motor car. My brother was nearly four years older than I was and had started school, so the treat was for myself and one or two other children of the same age, sitting stiffly and wordlessly beside the chauffeur or next to Lady Denman herself in the leather-and-petrol-reeking, though sumptuous, interior. To me it was bitterly disappointing. You could see so much from a trap, where you sat high up above the fields and hedges, which seemed to be snatched away from each side of the road as the horse pounded forward. Not quite as good as a trap, but better than kind Lady Denman's Daimler, was a ride home on the last cow when they were brought in for afternoon milking. You had to sit sideways because a cow's backbone is as sharp as a rail, and the view was limited, but the movement was delightful. The cow took not the slightest notice of me, but continued to chew as she walked. Ahead of us the majestic stomachs and udders of her companions swayed gently from side to side, and as they idled down the lane they left a trail of sweet grass-eater's breath.

We returned to London when I was five and a half. When I look back to my years in Sussex I have to tell myself that not everything was perfect. I was frightened of chained farm dogs, and still more of ganders. I didn't like Sussex bacon-and-suet pudding, which Mrs Ticehurst praised because it would stick to our ribs. Sometimes I was overwhelmed, standing in a field under an open blue sky, by a kind of terror at the enormity of the turning earth. I never remember feeling anything like that in London. But Balcombe was the place where for three years I had no real anxieties, and looked forward every night, as I fell asleep, to waking up the next day. My father was one of a large family, and he used to tell me that they were so happy in one of their homes (Kibworth Rectory in Leicestershire) that in later years they could always cure themselves of sleeplessness by thinking about it. I, too, if I can't sleep, think of Balcombe.

FREDERICK FORSYTH

Apart from a passing problem in my toddler days with one A. Hitler, Ashford was a good place to grow up. To the north was the Thames estuary coast, via ancient Canterbury, with all the wonders of cockling and whelking in the damp sands. To the east Folkestone and Dover played host to the steamers departing for that mysterious place, the Continent. North-west lay the old A20 to London, whither the bowler-hatted armies of clerks commuted each day from Ashford station, another amazing ritual, and to the south lay the dreaming Weald.

Ashford was a small and self-contained market town, its tradespeople, of which my parents were two, drawing their prosperity from the farming community on all sides. Every Tuesday the great cattle, sheep and pig market brought in the farmers, and their wives to do their shopping. It was the reason why so many of my father's friends were farmers, and their sons became mine.

Through that connection, the town boy

spent much of his growing years on the farms and developed an undying love and appreciation for that most beautiful artefact, the English countryside. With bicycle and sandwich pack I used to pedal through the Weald, between orchards of apple and pear and the endless fields of sweet-smelling hops. With my friends, John and David Cameron, I used to camp in the fields around their Woodchurch home, where we tried to survive on crow-egg omelettes.

This was Pop Larkin country, literally, for Marden, Smarden and Pluckley were the villages from which H.E. Bates, a close friend of my parents, drew his inspiration for those rustic novels, and where the TV series of *The Darling Buds of May* was filmed. It was a landscape of narrow lanes bordered by long grass and hedges, cowslip and parsley, where a boy could cycle in safety for miles, pulling into the grass only now and then to let a rattling Morris Minor go by.

Until I was about thirteen and went to boarding school, I think half that appeared on the family table was either grown, shot, picked or plucked from beneath a protesting hen.

There were shillings to be earned beating for the pheasant shoots at Bilsington Priory, and it was on the farms of Bob Hobbs at Smeeth and Ronnie Martin, a mile further on, that my father taught me to take rabbit and pigeon for the kitchen. Kent pigeon-breast pie is still a favourite.

There were the long, hot summers of the late Forties and early Fifties when my father would have a day off from the shop to take me rabbit-shooting at the time of reaping. There were millions of rabbits; the farmers were happy to have their numbers reduced and in the days of rationing they made a fine casserole. The ring of guns would stand round the edge of the wheat field as the clattering combine circled the uncut disc of wheat becoming smaller and smaller. Hiding in the stems the rabbits would wait until they panicked, then race for the hedge-row past the guns. Sometimes I would pick up half a truck-load before dusk.

There was a blacksmith at Willesborough, in whose dark forge we used to stand in awe as the barrel-chested smith pumped the horn-handled bellows with one had while holding the glowing horseshoe with tongs in the other, then plunging it deep into the white-hot coals before hammering it into shape on the anvil. I still recall my surprise when this hot metal was pressed into a raised hoof and the horse felt no pain.

There were discernible seasons then, and the foods that went with them. Winter brought turnips, swedes, beets and sprouts. Spring was for home-grown salads and summers – ah, the summers – brought strawberries gleaming under the sun on beds of ochre straw, and raspberries that went straight from the cane to the mouth. The birds took a lot, of course, for there were few if any pesticides or herbicides and nest-sites were everywhere so the land was noisy with birdsong. Between the insects, the birds and the schoolboys, it was a wonder anything ever got to market.

I know some will say that all the above is seen through rose-tinted specs. But I can testify that there were such summers, when to be a boy in short trousers with a bicycle in the Weald of Kent was to live in a place of endless activity and exploration; as Pop Larkin would say, just perfick.

CLARE FRANCIS

A suburban child, I dreamt only of the country. I was brought up first in Thames Ditton then in Esher, Surrey – both within easy commuting distance of London, where my father worked as a senior civil servant. Although mine was a happy home, and the houses themselves were pleasant enough, I never took to my surroundings, which I viewed with vague but unremitting dismay. In Thames Ditton I was disturbed by the immensity of suburbia, by its unrelieved monotony and lack of space. In Esher there was space of a self-conscious, carefully delineated sort, but our neighbours had a fortress mentality that precluded any sense of community, and the velvet lawns had a forbidding perfection.

If my dissatisfaction was precocious, it was because I had already found my spiritual home and it had spoiled me for anything else. Every Christmas, and some summers as well, my parents, my sister and I went to stay with my paternal grandparents in the

Yorkshire Dales. Up a narrow winding lane flanked by tall dry-stone walls, high above a distant plain, the White House stood in a pass of marginal farmland at the foot of a craggy hill topped by a limestone scar.

Built in 1753, the house had walls more than two feet thick and narrow mullioned windows. Inside, all was dark oak: the broad staircase with the grandfather clock whose tick echoed portentously through the house; the wide-planked floors blackened with polish; the high-backed settles on either side of the dining-room fire; the dark shining table laid for Christmas dinner.

A small house, it seemed large to me then. The cosy sitting-room of chintz and china that overlooked my grandmother's rock and water garden was not open to children, but when inside we preferred the kitchen anyway, for this was the centre of activities. There was no electricity, although a generator supplied spasmodic bursts of power. My grandmother would use flat irons heated on the range, expertly flicking water over the clothes with her free hand. She baked and roasted and conserved with only a marble-slabbed larder for refrigeration. The men would bring rabbits they had shot on the hill, and skin them in the large stone sink.

In those days, with rationing still a recent memory, my grandparents kept a clutch of goats and hens and the occasional pig. Ever since a large black hen had chased me across the croft I kept clear of the chickens and refused to collect their eggs. I did better with the goats, one of which I was allowed to milk; and once I had mastered the art of keeping the bucket upright I became quite proficient – although I never liked the milk itself, which was strong and sharp.

There were also guinea fowl, which laid their eggs rather cunningly in the stinging nettles; and, in summer, several hives of bees, which inhabited the walled vegetable garden. Peggy, a good-natured pony living rough in the hills for much of the year, used to take my sister and me on short rides, though I preferred the freedom of walking.

We would walk down the dark narrow lane at dust with empty pails to collect milk from the neighbouring farm. Better still was climbing the slope above the house and looking beyond the pass to the hills and the valley far below, where the steam trains trailed their smoke in puffballs across the landscape. There was nothing on the hill except rabbits, a few sheep and the sound of cascading water. The emptiness was like heaven to me.

A short way above the house a stream shot through the stone wall in a cataract and swirled into a pool overhung by a small rock. This was my secret place – at least I imagined it to be so. Here I would come in the wild and the wet when everyone else was inside, and lie on the rock looking down at the water. The fouler the weather, the better. I loved the rain on my face, the crashing water, the angry cawing of the rooks, the wind in the elms. I was never happier than when alone in that wild and beautiful place. In my writing I think I have been revisiting it ever since: all but one of my novels feature remote landscapes.

Christmas was the best time. Filling our stockings was no easy task for Father Christmas, who had to pick his way across the raised rafters in the floors of our attic bedroom. He sometimes stumbled and even, to our amazed delight, swore gently and giggled. In the early afternoon we ate goose and turkey, and fished for threepenny bits and silver sixpences in the plum pudding. In the evening, in the light of the oil lamps, charades were supervised with gusto by my grandmother, a keen amateur actress.

I have often wondered whether my memory has been especially selective, if the perfection was illusory. But I don't think so. Whenever I revisit the house, long since gone from the family, its magic never fails to touch me.

ANTONIA FRASER

One year in the life of a child is like a century. Certainly, the year/century that I spent at Water Eaton Manor, when I was seven years old, changed my whole perception of the world: not only did I encounter the country but I also found myself plunged into history – the reality of history.

It is true that in 1939, the country was not an entirely unknown experience. My eldest brother Thomas and I have eerie memories of staying with Aunt Caroline Pakenham, our great-great-aunt by marriage, at Bernhurst, her house in East Sussex. Aunt Caroline was the childless widow of a diplomat, Sir Frank Pakenham. Born in

1832, Uncle Frank had died in 1905 and my father had been named after him; it was understood that one day my father would inherit Bernhurst. That day, however, had been some time in coming.

By the time we knew Aunt Caroline, she was in her mid-nineties. Tiny, dressed in the fashions of Queen Victoria, she used a black parasol to emphasise her displeasure. Under the impression that, of us two, I was the boy, she would shout out imperiously: 'He fidgets! He fidgets!'

The pleasantest part of our memories concerned tea on the green velvet lawn. The butler would serve us, in stately fashion, having first trailed out a long flex in order to boil the kettle. Silver teapots always remind me of those gracious teas.

When my father inherited the house in June 1939, the lawn lost its green velvet hue, and there was no butler, let alone an electric kettle on a flex or a silver teapot. Only the view of Sussex remained the same: the Cézanne-like colours, the disposition of trees and hills that still enchants my parents nearly sixty years later. But Sussex was not at this point the family home, since my father worked as a don in Oxford; just a place to be enjoyed for holidays.

We were on holiday at Bernhurst in September 1939 when war broke out. Bernhurst turned out to be in a prohibited zone as it was only twelve miles from the coast. I have never forgotten that mammoth journey to Oxfordshire, not only because it took place in a taxi but also because Water Eaton Manor lay at the end of it. This Tudor house was on the banks of the River Cherwell, at the end of an extremely long drive – so long that we had the feeling of being completely cut off from the ordinary world during the year we lived there. Our presence, as evacuees, was due to the hospitable impulse of Lady (Teresa) Carr-Saunders, wife of the head of the London School of Economics, who decided to offer a refuge to two other families with young children. This meant that a nursery school could be established in one of the little lodges next to the big house.

A long time later, my mother told me that this was a time of anguish for the adults at Water Eaton, as the radio brought news of disasters daily, including the fall of France. All the same I could hardly believe her when she talked about the general misery. She was similarly astounded when I told her it was the happiest year of my (young) life and that for me, Water Eaton Manor was an enchanted place.

Lady Carr-Saunders contributed to this enchantment. Unlike my mother, Teresa Carr-Saunders adored the country, and was furthermore a formidably energetic farmer. She was not very tall, but made up for her lack of height with a character of great strength. I can still picture her, her abundant brown hair escaping from her bun, running out of the door with cries of dismay that the cows had escaped or the donkeys were in the vegetable garden.

The winter of 1939/40 was appalling, with thick snow and floods that turned the fields into one enormous flowing river. Once again, the grown-ups suffered while we children loved it, including the danger of wading through the waters.

Most importantly, Teresa Carr-Saunders was an ardent Catholic, from an ancient recusant family. The fact that Water Eaton contained a priest's hiding place inspired in me an interest in Catholic history that continues to this day. Teresa Carr-Saunders also set me off on another journey; when I was confirmed as a Catholic, many years later, I chose her as my godmother, and added Teresa to my baptismal name.

LESLEY GARRETT

It's only since I've grown older that I've realised how very extraordinary my childhood was. I have two amazing parents, very different people musically and in many other ways. My mum is a classical pianist. Her grandfather Wall was a miner, and he taught my granddad to play the piano out of a book, because he didn't want him to go down the pits. He became a successful concert pianist.

Added to that I had my wonderful father, whose family were much more in the light entertainment area. We were all taught, my two younger sisters and I, to play the piano and guitar, and to sing. That seemed to me to be a quite natural part of life. When I was a child, I didn't know anybody who didn't have a piano in their front room.

I was very precocious. I could talk before I was two. I could sing before that. My sister was born when I was a year and ten months old, and the midwife came the next day and said to me, 'Did you see what I brought you in my little black bag last night?' And I said, 'You didn't bring that, my mummy growed that.'

My dad wrote my first song for me around that time. It was called 'In the Deepest Jungle in Africa'. We have a recording of me doing it, so I know I could sing in tune from the beginning. I remember him lifting me up and sitting me on the piano with my legs dangling.

We sang 'Nessun Dorma', although we called it 'None Shall Sleep Tonight'; the 'Miserere' from *Il Travatore,* which we never had the English words for, so we just did it to La. I will remember that tune for ever; it is in my nappies, never mind my blood.

My parents had bought their first house the year before I was born, a little two-up-two-down derelict cottage, just outside Thorne in South Yorkshire, that my father painstakingly did up himself with my mother's help. They both worked on the railways before becoming teachers. But they did everything, plumbing, wiring, kitchens, and eventually bathrooms. Then they bought the one next door and knocked it through.

We had coal fires at home, no central heating. Until I was eleven we had tin baths in front of the fire and strip washes with a flannel. Ooh it tickled, until mum dried you.

The cottage was in a little hamlet, in a row of former dockworkers' cottages left over from when there was a prosperous port there on a bend in the River Don. All that was left was an oxbow lake. The abandoned hamlet was soon colonised by my family, when my mother's two sisters bought two more of the derelict cottages. The children roamed in gangs, sisters, cousins and lads from the farms. We played in the stack yards, in the river beds. We built rafts out of oil cans and planks.

There was a big pond at the end of the lake. One freezing winter day, near to Christmas, my sisters and I found two swans frozen into the ice. We thought one was still alive, so we tried to hack it out. I – terribly bossy – dispatched my sister back for the wheelbarrow. The fox had attacked and eaten its mate, which must have been a terrible experience for this poor animal.

I doubt now that it was alive, but we wanted to be heroines and heroes, so we wheeled it home to my patient mum and dad. They tried to get it going, and played along completely. Eventually they broke it to us very gently that the swan was already dead. I cried for hours and hours.

Winters were terribly hard then and we went ice skating every year.

We couldn't wait for Christmas one year, when we were about six, five and three. We were so desperate for new toys, my dad got fed up and said, 'Oh, for goodness sake have some stilts!'

He was constantly building and renovating, so there was plenty of wood lying around. He nailed a couple of bits together, a pair for each of us. We loved those bits of wood so much we went all over his setting concrete in them – which made him cross. Then Christmas came, and we got our toys, and we were very excited. On Boxing Day we said, 'Where are our stilts?' Dad said, 'I've burnt them. I didn't think you would want them now you've got all your presents.' It was our turn to be cross with him.

Our house was full of music and family at Christmas. We went carol singing, and I sang in the choir at school. At junior school I had to go to the back, because the teacher said she couldn't hear anyone else. At senior school I always sang solos because I had a really big voice.

I had a rich childhood because of my parents. They were very free-thinking for the times, in the things they would allow us to do. Particularly my father, to the point of recklessness. He let me light a fire by myself when I was eight. He is a great one for children learning by experience. He got a bit more twitchy when I got into adolescence. I remember saying at sixteen or seventeen, 'Why don't you just let me go on the Pill?' He hit the roof.

If I had to sum up my childhood in one word, it would be rubble. One night, my mum and dad were arguing in bed about who should put out the light. In the end, my dad reaching down and picked up the nearest bit of rubble – half a brick – and threw it at the light bulb. End of argument.

RUMER GODDEN

My childhood was as halcyon as it was unusual. Our father, Fa, was an agent for India's Inland Navigation so that we (our mother, Mam, my three sisters, Jon, Nancy and Rose, and I) lived on the banks of

Assam's and Bengal's great rivers, sometimes two miles wide, flowing through land so flat that it seemed to meet the sky all round like an inverted bowl. If there is any space in me it comes from that sky.

Though I was born in Sussex I went out to India at six months old. We travelled back and forth between England and India until I was seven when, because of the First World War, we did not leave India for five idyllic years from 1915.

In Bengal our town Narayanganj's river was the Lakya, part of the vast network of the Brahmaputra and the only direct way into the town. There was plenty of life in and on the river: a life of crocodiles and fish, of porpoises that somersaulted in and out of the water, of herons and egrets wading in the shallows and kingfishers perched on the marker posts. Steamers sent waves up the banks and naked brown boys jumped into the wash, shouting and laughing.

Ferries, loaded to the gunwales, went from bank to bank; a cluster of buffaloes being washed by small boys lay contentedly in the shallows. Sometimes a marigold garland from a festival or a funeral floated past, or the corpse of a kid, swollen with water; sometimes there was a whole dead cow with

72

a vulture perched on it. The river took them *all* away.

I suppose ours was a monstrous house, a great, rectangular, pale-grey stucco house, standing on a high plinth that was hidden by plumbago and a hedge of poinsettias. Stone-arched, green-shuttered verandahs ran the full length of the two floors. The roof was flat, with a high parapet that was cut into loopholes. Double steps, banked with pots of budding chrysanthemums, led up from the drive. White-dressed, white-turbanned servants went in and out. In front of the house was an enormous cork tree covered in white blossom every spring; the flower bed round its base held amaryllis lilies. Every morning at sunrise and every evening at sunset a flag was run up or down the flagstaff on our roof. It was the company flag but we thought it was Fa's.

Some people would say we were deprived. There were no European schools in Narayanganj so that I did not go to school until I was twelve; Jon was fourteen. We were taught at home by Mam's maiden sister, Aunt Mary, who had not been to school herself. How shocking; but I have always thanked God I did not have 'sensible' parents.

In those days in the long 'hot weather',

women and children were sent out of the heat to the hills. Sensible parents would have chosen a hill station near us, rented a house, and sent us every year to the same school. Mam chose instead to take us to a different hill station every year so that we travelled the length and breadth of India, from Kashmir in the far north-west, four days' journey by train and road, to the Nilgiri Hills in the south. In other years it was Shillong in Assam, Mussooree near Simla, and Darjeeling.

We travelled through the scorched aridness of the Scinde desert, lived in the Himalayas facing the peaks of snow, saw cities and mud-walled villages. We picked gentians and edelweiss in Kashmir and hibiscus and bougainvillea in our own garden. We knew palm trees and jungle thorn trees, and the temple frangipani with its fragrant chiselled flowers, as we knew peach, plum and cherry blossom; and birds from flamingoes, peacocks and the brain-fever birds to bulbuls and hoopoes.

Our house was a mingling of religions: Hannah, the ayah, was a Thomist Catholic; the table servants were Mohammedan; Fa's personal bearer, Jetta, was a Buddhist from

Sikkim. The gardeners were Hindu Brahmins of the highest caste; the sweeper, also Hindu, an Untouchable. All lived together in contentment.

I suppose things made such indelible impressions on us because we had so little. In that faraway Bengali town there were no European shops, certainly no bookshops; we had books, but few, so we wrote our own. All of us wrote; poems and stories poured out of us. It was a good thing, as Fa said, that the house had so many wastepaper baskets.

Of course it had to end; in March 1920 we sailed from Calcutta. It was a grey, chill, rainy spring morning when the ship berthed at Plymouth. Everything was grey, wet and colourless as we stood by the rail watching the luggage being unloaded into the customs sheds. A sailor set Hathi, a small stuffed elephant on wheels, on the luggage chute; Hathi had come with us because no one could imagine our youngest sister, Rose, without him. Wearing his scarlet flannel pad, he rolled majestically down the chute to the quay and everybody laughed and cheered.

Jon and I did not cheer, for a cold realisation was creeping over us. This was the end of our childhood. Soon even Rose would not want toys anymore.

NIGEL HAVERS

Passed between Suffolk and London, my childhood has given me a huge love of England, of both its countryside and capital. But it was in the countryside that I spent most time and where most of my memories remain. The area around Ousden, near Newmarket, where we had a family home, was a haven for wildlife, a rich mixture of hills, fertile fields and beckoning woods.

Suffolk is a county seldom used as a through route, and I remember Ousden for its rambling walks, its ponds abundant with fish, and the mini clock tower – almost a replica of Big Ben and designed by the same architect – marking its centre. After driving for hours on winding roads from London – where my father Sir Michael Havers, QC practised – we would be welcomed by its country smells, followed by an even more desirable aroma of roast lamb cooking in the kitchen.

It was not always that way. My earliest

memory is of having my bath in a tub at the old thatched cottage which my parents had just bought. I must have been five. Uninhabited for around 200 years, the cottage had no running water or electricity. Weekend after weekend was spent renovating what, at first, resembled an old barn. As the years passed, additions were made until the house became a string of rooms leading into one another, log fires in every one. Perfect for entertaining; Friday nights were legendary, with friends and neighbours, lawyers and politicians, throwing opinions across the dinner table, a potential battlefield. But it was croquet that inspired the most serious family rows, resulting in many a silent dinner.

A gardening fanatic, my father planted 500 or 600 trees on our four acres of lawns, producing a paradise for tree climbers. The variety of vegetables he grew required the assistance of two gardeners, one of whom lived in a small house attached to our land. I once ate the first ripe tomato of the year as I wandered past one of the greenhouses, only to meet a very angry father who had been waiting for weeks to consume it himself. August would conclude most of his year's work, with produce ripened to perfection. Ironically, August is also the month that the courts don't sit, and my father's only chance to take a holiday. The fact that he was never able to reap his rewards became a family joke.

Despite the endless days spent helping Dad ploughing and digging with whatever latest gadget was his whim, whole sections of the gardens were left completely untouched and were the only parts with many flowers. Uncultivated land had strict rules: bending rather than snapping branches that got in the way, not squashing insects and preserving the environment for birds to live and breed.

Barns and outhouses among the gardens made for wonderful play, although there was one fewer than there should have been, thanks to my burning it down, by accident, at the ripe old age of six. One shelter, with a full-sized billiard table, became a landmark of my childhood and my older brother Philip's. But it was outdoor activity that was to have the most lasting effect. I learned to play golf at seven, and to ride shortly afterwards. Football, cricket, tennis – they were all favourites, but then we played any game we could get our hands on. Newmarket meant horse racing, another great pastime. Philip was the ultimate organiser with something planned for every day. Many a night we fished in the village pond with days spent shooting pigeons for farmers. We used to shoot pheasants and rabbits to eat, but pigeons were notoriously challenging for they can see you from miles away. There was a time when one farmer offered a shilling for every bird.

I attended a boarding school in Bury St Edmunds with Philip from the age of six. Run by two brothers and a sister, everyone – including the headmaster – was called by their Christian name. It was there, taking part in the annual Shakespeare plays, that I discovered my ability to act. *A Winter's Tale* was the first play I performed in, and *A Midsummer Night's Dream* – a magical production with a mixture of adults and children and me as Puck – the best.

Sadly, when my father became Attorney General, our family home, surrounded by police and electric fences, seemed to lose its character. But Suffolk – with its superb landscapes and the greatest bitter in the country – hasn't changed a bit.

THORA HIRD

I was born in Morecambe, Lancashire, on a Sunday, when the church bells were ringing. My brother, Neville, was born on a Sunday, when the church bells were ringing. He was born just before Morning Service and I was born just before Evening Service. Not on the same Sunday, of course. He appeared twenty-one months before me. I think this was so that he could look the world over, approve it and make sure that it was safe for 'our kid', 'George' or 'Horace'. These were the names he called me. I can't think why. I am very proud of being extremely feminine.

I remember the love and devotion that shone in my mother's eyes when she recalled the church bells. As a little girl, I felt they had rung because Neville and I had been born. I used to swank at school about the church bells bit – not in a clever clogs voice but in a rather grateful way.

I wasn't born in a bunk, a theatrical skip or a hamper. I was born comfortably and snugly, in bed. I made my first appearance on the boards at the tender age of eight weeks old. My mother was appearing in a drama as the young heroine who had been 'done wrong' by the squire's son. I played the unfortunate result. My father was the director (or the producer, as they were called in those days). That was the first and only part I ever got through influence. And I slept during the entire proceedings.

Earlier in their marriage, my parents had decided to stay put instead of touring all over England, Wales and Scotland. They had made a permanent home for themselves in Morecambe. My father became stage manager on the West End Pier, and then he ascended another rung of the ladder when he became stage manager at The Alhambra. Years afterwards, it was used for the film *The Entertainer* with Laurence Olivier.

From The Alhambra my father moved upwards again, to become stage manager of The Royalty Theatre. The house next door, at 6 Cheapside, went with the job. Of course, at this point, I wasn't even a gleam in his eye. I still smile when I recall my mother telling me how, after six years of marriage, they were *delighted* to discover a baby was on the way. That was Olga. And how, fifteen months later, they were *delirious* that another was expected. That was Neville. A year after Neville was born, they were *demented* to find that yet another baby was due. And that was me: Thora Hird, of 6 Cheapside, Morecambe, Lancashire, England, Europe, The World! I would write that on my things – on the flyleaf of my Schoolgirl Diary, on my Sunday School prizes (always books), on the inside flap of my leather school bag and on the bottom of my varnished wood pencil box.

I grew out of the 'Europe' and 'The World' bit by the time I was about nine. But I'm quite sure it was only because I would have been satisfied – no, proud – to have gone through life with just one word after my name: Cheapside. I loved it! I enjoyed the sound of the word Cheapside. Not Cheapside Street, or Road or Avenue or Drive or Crescent. Just Cheapside. There was a great sound of authority about it, added to which there was the number of our house. Six. The number six went with the word Cheapside better than any other number. I would have been deprived of a lot of private pleasure had I been born at, let us say, number 2 or number 11, or 28 or 31. Our side of Cheapside was the three front steps and bay window side. The residents of the other side with an odd number (unfortunate souls), had only one step and a flat, ordinary window.

Neville and I almost lived in the theatre. We were taught all sorts of little jobs by the permanent stage-hands: how to work the curtain, how to cleat a flat. In case that sounds foreign, cleating a flat means fastening two pieces of scenery (two flats) together with a piece of rope that is thrown over a hook (the cleat) and tied into a figure of eight knot. Is it any wonder that I entered the theatrical profession? (Neville didn't. He went to college and became an electrical engineer.) But I did. Although my parents begged me to do something else, they weakened eventually and taught me all I know about 'play acting'.

When I was ten years old I was May Queen of the school. The school I attended was the Preparatory School, Morecambe, run by Misses Elizabeth and Merci Nelson. I cannot speak highly enough of them or their teachings: good manners, good English, good handwriting and, added to all that, honesty and love.

Before the May Queen elections, a blackboard was put up in the classroom. On it was written: 'When you vote for the May Queen of this school, remember: Not the wittiest one. Or the prettiest one. Nor she with the gown most gay. But she who is pleasantest all the day through. With the kindest of things to say and to do. *She* shall be Queen of the May.'

Well, pardon my blushes, but one year I was elected. My mother made me a beautiful coronation dress out of one of her evening gowns. The crown was made of ordinary field daisies but they were so beautiful. I wore white buckskin shoes and my hair had been put up in white linen curl rags the night before.

Unfortunately, on the day, it rained. So the whole production was held in the school. Chairs were hastily placed in rows for the parents (mine were in the middle of the front row, of course); school tables and boxes made a 'royal hill' at the end of the big classroom; Miss Nelson's chair from behind her desk was used as a throne and the entire set was covered with a massive green cloth.

By the middle of the maypole dancing my curls and the daisy crown were beginning to droop a bit – but it didn't make me feel any less regal. Then suddenly the back leg of the throne slipped off the box it stood on and the Queen fell down sideways. The six Maids of Honour, the headmistress and various others had to assist Her Most Gracious Majesty to get up. Unhurt, but a bit shaken, she was trying not to cry. My mother and father were looking lovingly concerned, when Mother broke into a little laugh. I knew why and, with an effort, I laughed too. Soon the room was in uproar, my throne was replaced and, crown awry, so was I. My mother, the actress, had given me my first lesson: the show must go on.

ELIZABETH JANE HOWARD

My childhood country was the borders of East Sussex and Kent. We did not live there, but spent all the holidays there: first staying with my grandparents in a house near Battle (the Home Place I have written about in my Cazalet Chronicles novels), and later about five miles away in a house called The Beacon that my grandfather acquired for his sons and their descendants.

Home Place lay halfway down a hill, at the bottom of which ran a stream. Behind the house was a small wood, and beyond that large meadows fringed by a more serious wood. The place and its surroundings imprinted themselves deeply, so that even now, sixty years later, I can think back to any part of it with the utmost clarity and ease. I think this kind of memory is true for most people, and the chief reason for it is that when one is a child one can be deeply appreciative and perceptive of smells, sights and sounds, but one doesn't talk about them to other people; in a sense that would be giving a piece of them away. So one simply *has* all that sensation and it gets stored whole, inside.

In my youth that part of Sussex was lush and green, with good woods and streams that had not been dammed or polluted or piped underground. The lanes were winding and extremely narrow, with immensely high banks that in spring and summer were covered with primroses, wild strawberries, scarlet pimpernel, speedwell, stitchwort, little brilliant ferns and dog violets. The woods – some of them – smoked with blue-bells at Easter, and wood anemones, celandine and lady's-smock abounded. The meadows had poppies, ox-eye daisies and cow parsley, and in autumn horse mushrooms could be collected by the trugful. Across the road from Home Place lay seemingly endless hop fields, geometric, aromatic. 'Hop pillows make you sleep,' they said, and I imagined a million pillows being made every year before I knew about beer.

The Beacon, the house in which most of my holiday childhood was spent, was very different. There we led a more spartan life. The house stood on a hill, hence its name; it was reputed to be on the site of one of the beacons lit to warn the English of the Norman invasion. Because of the hill it was very short of water (we were not on any mains). It had a well that regularly ran dry in summer. A bath was a rare and heavily populated occasion, and we mostly made do with swimming in the sea and having a bucket of water chucked over us in the evenings on the lawn. We fetched drinking water from a spring near Home Place.

I cannot imagine how nannies coped with nappy and baby clothes washing, nor can I think how our gardener's wife – the cook – managed to make meals for upwards of twenty-five people on an ancient, intractable kitchen range. There was no fridge or even ice, but a larder with remnants of food on a slate slab. Flypapers hung from hooks in the ceiling and became encrusted with flies, like vast jet chokers. Milk arrived twice a day in a steaming bucket from Mr York's farm. The only heating in the house came from two or three log fires.

In the late summer the King of the Gipsies came, with a large entourage: beautifully painted wagons, barefooted children, enticing dark ladies in full skirts and flowered blouses with scarlet kerchiefs on their heads and gold earrings in daytime (not something commonly to be seen on one's mother or aunts). They spoke Romany, and were the ones the men sent to the kitchen door to sell clothes pegs and baskets. There were always spare ponies and lurchers tied to the back of the wagons.

They were the most exciting people I had ever seen. They stole, the servants said: geese, rabbits, eggs, apples, vegetables, plums, anything they could lay their hands on. Occasionally it crossed my mind that it would be lovely to be stolen by them, but from the books I read they seemed only to go in for babies.

Expeditions were few and repetitive – not something that children mind in the least.

We went to the beach at Cooden, at Bexhill, and, more enjoyably, Camber Sands and Pett Level. The sand there made a welcome change from painful pebbles, and Pett Level combined wonderful rock pools with quantities of bottle glass that we used to collect with fervour.

We used to go to Bodiam Castle with a picnic lunch. It is the perfect castle for a child, as it is more or less intact, can be thoroughly explored, and has a proper moat. But its glamour diminished for me when I discovered that it had never been inhabited.

When the war came my grandfather decreed that everyone was to dig an air raid shelter. This included very small people with wooden spades. Later, as our house was right in the fairway for enemy aircraft on their way to London, he said it must be camouflaged. It was white roughcast, but after much family effort it was covered with slabs and whorls of dark salmon-pink, sky-blue and pea-green paint. (The only colours available? I cannot believe they were *chosen.*). At any rate, but the time we had finished we must have provided the Luftwaffe with the most reliable landmark they were ever likely to have.

JENNIFER JOHNSTON

I love to wave at trains as they rattle past. It is almost an automatic response to raise my hand in greeting as the engine passes, pulling behind it its long snake of carriages. Nowadays no one waves back. They are too engrossed in eating from plastic bags.

They used to wave.

They used to look out of the windows of trains at the landscape and wave at children standing below on the beach or waiting with their bikes at level-crossing gates. I always used to like that momentary connection with people going somewhere else, passing to and fro, people in motion.

The small seaside town about eighteen miles south of Dublin, where I spent my summers until I was old enough to make decisions for myself, had a neat and handsome little station. Until the middle of the last century, Greystones had been a fishing village of just a few houses snuggled round a stone pier. Then the railway company that had built the line down the east coast from Dublin to Wexford decided to build a station there.

The whole nature of the village changed then, as acres of substantial villas were built and bought by members of the Dublin professional classes who transported their households there for sunny weekends and the long summer holidays.

My maternal grandparents had such a villa: a charming house full of light, surrounded by a huge garden, orchard, tennis court and croquet lawn. A high escallonia hedge protected us from our neighbours ... or, on reflection, our neighbours from us, for we were a rowdy lot.

My grandfather left the house to his eldest daughter, my aunt, on the understanding that all family members could spend their holidays there. So every summer through the Thirties and Forties, it held a motley rabble of babies, teenagers, students, nannies and helpers, over whom my aunt reigned with apparent calmness. She was a formidable woman with whom you did not argue, but she had a sense of fair play that didn't, it seemed to me, necessarily exist in other grown-ups.

The wide beach was about 300 yards from our house, down a narrow road and through and archway under the railway line. If you stood under the arch when a train passed overhead you could see, through the cracks in the wooden supports, the flash of metal as the wheels turned.

As you ran into the sea, the gritty sand gave way to small, sharp pebbles. On turbulent days the waves flung the pebbles against your legs and caused stinging abrasions, out of which you often had to pick little bits of stone. On good days the sea was blue with a sparkling icy brightness. On bad days it was grey, like the clouds, wrapping us all in a chiaroscuro chill.

In between golf, going to the races and gardening, my aunt taught us all to swim. This was wartime across the water; many of the children playing on the beach had fathers, and sometimes mothers, fighting in the War. They had come to Greystones to live with aunts or grandparents who also felt impelled to teach their charges to swim. There was no escape for the faint-hearted. It was as if a duty had been imposed by the presence of war and the absence of parents.

A long row of bathing boxes stood in hierarchical order below the railway line. They held dry towels, rugs, bathing shoes (worn only by grown-ups), tins of ginger biscuits, old tennis rackets for playing rounders and inflatable rubber rings, which we were not allowed to use. We had to swim! Competitions were held to see who could jump the furthest off the tall boxes, until grown-ups, exasperated by the flying sand, chased us away.

Then we would run along the tracks, balancing on the rails or hopping from sleeper to sleeper, until we came to a distant point where huge granite blocks heaped on the shore acted as a bulwark against winter seas. These blocks became for us caves, castles, pirate ships and mountain crags. There, with no one to hear or see us, or try to teach us to swim, we lived a free and glorious life.

It was the passing of the 12.30 train down to Wicklow that brought us back to reality. After waving to the driver, who would whistle cheerfully back, and then to the passengers, we would head, barefoot and sandy, for our various homes, along the once more empty tracks: to be late for lunch was as great a crime as refusing to learn to swim.

VINNIE JONES

I was brought up on a council estate on the outskirts of Watford in Hertfordshire, but we were right on the edge of the country. We lived just off the end of a lane, where Dad worked on a small shoot. He was the shoot captain – he looked after the birds and organised the running of it. I wouldn't like to say exactly where it was because it's still there today and shoots get problems if you so much as mention them.

Funnily enough, Dad wasn't born a country person, but he got into all the country sports and lived for his shooting. He was a builder by trade. He had his own firm, then packed it in to become a full-time gamekeeper. As a kid, I spent most of my time on his shoot. In the school holidays my mates and I took a tent and stayed down there. We practically lived there, setting traps, working our ferrets and just enjoying running about in the fresh air.

I feel very sorry for kids now. You see them hanging out on street corners, looking bored, and then there are all the drugs around. It's tough for them. I don't know if there were drugs about in our day. There may have been, but we were always out in the woods. Looking back on my own childhood, it was an innocent time. It was certainly a great time. For holidays we went to Butlins, or fishing in Ireland. One of my clearest memories is catching a huge pike there with my sister, Ann. I must have been eight or nine at the time.

I was always very interested in fishing and shooting. Dad taught me the ropes and I learned by going out with him and a .410 shotgun. I shot my first pigeon on a trip with him. We had been out decoying on the stubbles and this pigeon came in. I can still remember the thrill I felt – the closest I can get to describing it now would be scoring a goal. I was five. My first fish was more of a cheat. Dad and I went fishing on Gratham Water, near Huntingdon. We hadn't had any luck, but on the way back to the car we spotted a fish lying by the track, then another, and another. We just followed this line of fish; they must have dropped out of someone's bag on the way back to the car park. Dad said it seemed a shame to waste them, so we picked them up and took them home with us.

Sometimes I had a terrible time at school over the shooting. We'd do these topics in class; I'd do mine on shooting, and then get into arguments about it. Even then, I realised people were arguing about something they didn't properly understand and that's what really got up my nose. It still does.

Most of my mates weren't particularly interested in shooting but they were certainly interested in the money they could get from it. We'd go off beating for my Dad and earn a bit of cash. I saved up my beating money to buy my first gun, a Baikal over-and-under. I was fifteen, but it was really getting to the stage where the shooting clashed something terrible with my football. Dad would stop me going beating in order to concentrate on the football. It was very hard sometimes.

I can't remember a time when I wasn't playing football. I learned as soon as I could walk. It was a natural part of life. All us young lads played football – I was just better than any of the others. I captained the school team, then got picked for the Watford Boys. What I enjoyed about it was what I enjoyed about the shooting – the competitiveness.

I had a happy childhood up until my parents got divorced, then we all rather went our separate ways. One of my best times was a year spent working as a gamekeeper on an estate near St Albans. I did it partly to help Dad out, but I had a great time rearing 4,000 pheasants on my own. I was just coming up to sixteen, and to have that much responsibility was good for me. At that time, it looked like it was going to be a toss-up between whether I'd be a footballer or a gamekeeper. The football won but, even today, I still think of my trade as keepering. I could be a gamekeeper again tomorrow.

When I was growing up, I never really thought of myself as a country or town person, but now I realise I know much more about the countryside. I think I understand it. As a kid, I always knew more about the names of animals and birds than I ever did about night-clubs. Now I'm living in the country again and my son's being brought up there, I suppose I've come full circle. The country gets deep in you: I thought that recently when I was invited to Gazza's wedding. I didn't go. I knew there'd be too many rooks to see to at that time.

FERGAL KEANE

My first country memory is of an afternoon in high summer and me riding with my cousin Willie Purtill on a donkey and cart along a laneway thick with fuchsia and brambles. I must have been about six years old and we were returning from the creamery at Lissleton. An empty milk churn sat between us and Willie tapped his fingers methodically on the metal casing. His other hand held the reins and from time to time he clicked his tongue, a reminder to the ancient donkey that we were there. Around us the farmland of north Kerry stretched from Cnoc on Oir (the Mountain of Gold) down to the Atlantic Ocean at Ballybunion. We could sniff the sea scent mingling with the smell of hay and ripe blackberries.

Our people had farmed here for genera-tions, through war and famine and rebellion and finally peace. They were small farmers who had known hard times but I doubt that they ever regarded themselves as poor. Half-way down the lane we reached a thatched building and Willie pulled hard on the reins to stop the donkey. 'Wait here awhile, boyo,' he said to me. After a few minutes Willie returned with a tin mug filled to the brim with a foaming black substance. 'Would you like a sup of porter?' he asked. 'What's porter?' I replied. 'It's a kind of drink,' he said. I lifted the mug and took a long gulp of warm, bitter liquid. I loved it.

Thus did I make the acquaintance of Guinness, a substance with which I would eventually form an abiding friendship. That was also the summer I first milked a cow, the warm milk spraying across my sandals while old Madge Purtill clucked away behind me. 'Aim for the bucket, boy, aim for the bucket,' she called out.

I was an early convert to the magic of the Irish countryside. Back then it was still a place in thrall to old traditions and mythologies. The power of the Catholic Church was absolute but beneath the cloak of Christian morality lurked older, more elemental forces. Greatest of these was the intense passion for land. My uncle once described watching farmers tenderly running their fingers through ears of corn on a late summer's day. 'It was like seeing a man run his hand through the hair of a beautiful woman,' he said. Men killed for the love of land and no power on earth or in heaven would dare come between them and the loam of a north Kerry field.

From those long-ago summers I remember the beach at Ballybunion where the tinkers sold sacks of dried seaweed and periwinkles and where I first rode a horse. The memory is seared into my consciousness. For halfway through the ride my younger cousin Conor came creeping up behind the poor animal and smacked it hard on the rump. The horse took off at a fierce gallop in the direction of the cliffs, halted only by an extraordinary bellow from its owner. I howled piteously and was treated to a candy floss. My cousin had his ears boxed.

At night we listened to ghost stories in my grandmother's kitchen where an open range served both as fire and cooker. My father mixed Irish legends with local folklore and we listened wide-eyed with fright as the country night drew near in shadows.

My most deep-rooted memories of north Kerry are those connected with my father. People familiar with my writing will know of my father's long and unsuccessful struggle with alcohol. Often that battle was fought on family holidays. But I would prefer to remember him as he was on one of our better days in the country. We had spent the afternoon on the River Feale fishing for trout. Our only catch was a small creature barely big enough for the pan. But the size did not matter.

My father who had never changed a plug or done a single practical thing had shown me a secret skill. We walked home through Gurtenard Woods, me running after him and around him and in front of him. When we reached the main street with the tea-time lights coming on in every house, I made him take the little fish out of the bag and hold it in front of us. I was proud of him all right. Father and son, in the heart of the country.

SARAH KENNEDY

'You won't fit in,' our Surrey relatives chorused the minute my parents announced that we were moving from Wallington into the countryside near East Grinstead, Sussex. How would we manage without street lights?

But of course I, my two sisters, Anne and

Jane, and brother Richard took to it like ducks to water. Aged ten, I found it terribly exciting to live up a lovely, unmade road in a house that backed on to open fields. Less exciting perhaps for my father, who had to commute up and down to London and kept getting punctures as he drove to the station.

Nearby, at Haywards Heath, Aunty Vera and Uncle Clarence lived in an old Victorian house. We thought they were incredibly grand. The house had everything: a butler's pantry; a huge range in the kitchen which the maid, Alice, used to black, and milk churns in the scullery.

It was a wonderful place – a fairy world. After a lunch with delicacies such as asparagus that we could never afford because Mummy and Daddy had the four of us, the deckchairs would be put out in the garden and Alice would bring tea. Home-made cakes, a little group of midges and cows mooing in the field – it's always summer in childhood memories.

It was there that I learnt how to milk by hand. Aunty Vera kept a herd of Jersey cows with great liquid eyes. It was a thrill to see the milk foaming into the bucket and smell the cow pressed against you.

We had animals – dogs, cats and donkeys.

Our first dog was Traddles, a yellow Labrador, but he was so uncontrollable that we had to give him away to the local pub where he was in his element. And Wonky, the Siamese cat, got into the pantry one Christmas and ate half the turkey. Mother managed to stuff it so it almost looked whole and we ate it after all. You wouldn't do that now, would you? The donkeys, Crumpet and Sancho, lived in a field at the bottom of the garden. Crumpet was wicked and would take offence at people. Unfortunately, he took agin my Aunt Hello Dear (every time she sees me she says 'Hello Dear'). We were setting off for a walk across their field. Crumpet took one look at Aunt Hello Dear's well-padded bottom, rushed across the field and bit a very large chunk out of it, coat and all.

My mother taught us to be responsible about keeping animals. I have found memories of her speech as we returned home after a day out: 'Now, Sarah, you feed the donkeys. Anne, you do the cats...': a constant stream of tasks. Having animals also introduced us to the tougher side of country life. Aged twelve, I used to help a neighbour, Mrs Quilter, look after her chickens. Of course, the inevitable happened and one day a fox got in the hen house. Even now I can't look at a chicken without remembering the carnage. I am terribly squeamish but my mother was practical. Once I found, to my horror, a sheep's head on the Aga. Money was tight and Mother was cooking it for the dogs.

We went on summer holidays to Swanage in Dorset. Some days the rain would come down in ribbons and we'd be crammed in the Morris Minor with the windows steamed up. Daddy would sit there rattling *The Daily Telegraph*, while Mother would peer up at the sky and say optimistically, 'I think it is clearing up.'

Other years we'd go to Cornwall or Wales where we mucked about in boats. We stubbed our toes, ran around in wet, sandy costumes and drank from a Thermos of soup. We stayed in a guest house which felt terribly grand. Things were tight – orangeade was a luxury. I remember my mother saying, 'Other people can afford it, but we're doing all right on water.'

When I was twelve we moved to a house at Copthorne, near Gatwick airport. In those days about two planes a day landed. We had a vegetable patch, which fascinated me, and a gardener called Jack. One day I asked him whether he preferred flowers or vegetables. He replied, 'I hate herbaceous stuff because you can't eat it.' Today, I love Warwickshire, where I escape to my country cottage, for that same down-to-earth quality.

The country of my childhood cast a spell on me. When I lived in Germany and the Far East I became a fanatic of *The Archers*: it was my route back to the English countryside. Now I find my cottage is the only place where I relax. Every Friday, I cannot wait to get there. My heart lifts as I leave the lights of London behind. And then the next morning I wake to the sound of horses trotting past.

LYNDA LA PLANTE

I had the best of all worlds as a child. I lived close to the seaside, at Blundellsands near Liverpool, and near marvellous countryside, too. It was a childhood of scrambles and picnics, bike rides and inventive games. Television was not allowed to dominate – I can hardly recall any children's television programmes apart from *Top of the Pops*, but I can remember as if it were yesterday the day of the Sniggery Woods picnic.

My very best friend was called Alison. She was tiny, with bright eyes, rosy cheeks and curly blonde hair. Then there was Jane, who had that white blonde, dead straight hair, and Victoria, who I was very envious of because she had a drop handlebar bicycle.

My gang had been working on a play I had written, and I decided we should rehearse it in the woods. The play was similar to *Cinderella* and I was delighted when Jane led me to a large wicker basket in her garage and revealed all the costumes for the local amateur dramatics production of *Camelot*.

We removed three gowns, three cone-shaped hats and a man's doublet and hose. We determined some alterations might be necessary, so Jane fetched a pair of scissors and we stuffed the gowns into bin bags. Flushed with excitement, we packed up and wobbled off on our bikes with lemonade, sandwiches and apples to Sniggery Woods.

Panting and gasping, we pushed our way along a dirt track until we found a suitable location. The ground was carpeted with bluebells and the tall trees guarded the small clearing, making it feel cool, silent and magical. After we'd eaten and polished off the lemonade we all stripped off and tried on the costumes. The gowns were too long and after an in-depth discussion and a few arguments – Victoria didn't want to play Buttons but she was the tallest – we began the 'alterations'.

According to my mother, I've been lethal with a pair of scissors all my life. As Alison stood on a tree stump, I hacked round the bottom of her pale blue draped gown. Next I took a few inches off all the hats. Victoria, still miffed at having to play the man, said we looked like dwarfs, but, with her yellow tights knotted and jammed into her shoes and the doublet looking better with the sleeves cut off, she had to admit the end result was pretty satisfying and the rehearsal began.

Meanwhile, the local amateur dramatic society was preparing for its dress rehearsal of *Camelot*. Jane's mother, the wardrobe mistress, loaded the skip into her car and departed for the town hall.

We were blissfully unaware of time. Victoria was getting well into her stride as the Prince searching for his lost love; Alison, the prettiest of us all, lay as if dead among the bluebells; Jane and I were wicked stepmothers.

The *Camelot* dress rehearsal was in uproar. The leading lady and ladies-in-waiting had no costumes, nor did the director (who doubled as an actor). Jane's mother returned home. By now it was 5.30pm and she was beginning to worry about the whereabouts of her daughter, never mind the missing costumes.

Victoria, with a stick for a sword, had been waiting for her moment, stuck in a tree, for half an hour, and was becoming very impatient. The rehearsal began to disintegrate as Jane wanted to leave. It was getting dark and only Victoria had a light on her bicycle, so we started to change out of the costumes.

Jane began to cry. It was the jagged pieces of material that set her off and the realisation that they couldn't instantaneously be put back together. I was very firm with her: we would simply replace the costumes in the skip and nobody would know. Little Alison agreed – she always agreed with me – but Victoria had to put her ten cents' worth in.

'They might, you know, Lynda. They're all a couple of feet shorter.' We then collapsed in giggles as Victoria still had on the cut-down tights with the knot in the foot and looked ridiculous.

Meanwhile, *Camelot* was due to open the following night, and there were still no costumes for the leading players. Everyone was beginning to get hysterical. Jane's mother was beside herself. She called Alison's mother, who called Victoria's mother, who called mine.

'Oh, I think they've gone to Sniggery Woods,' my mother said.

'They wouldn't have taken the costumes for *Camelot*, would they?'

My mother hesitated and said they should all get going as fast as possible, asking nonchalantly if anyone had any scissors missing.

The bike riders pedalled back the quick way via the small country lanes, while the mothers drove to the woods along the main road. They had to climb over fences and wade through a sea of nettles before eventually discovering the evidence left strewn in the bluebell dell.

Our mothers sat up all night, sewing back the sleeves and the hems, and *Camelot* opened on time. Jane was forbidden ever to see me again; Victoria and Alison were not allowed out for a month, and I was duly punished. Then it was school again; summer was over.

I never did return to Sniggery Woods, but they will remain for ever imprinted on my mind as part of my childhood. I will always remember little Alison in the blue gown, lying on a bed of bluebells. She died of leukaemia when she was twelve. My headmistress died the same year. Strange the things you remember: I had a bunch of pussy willows for my headmistress, which I'd cut from the fields by our house. Miss Ashley stood outside the gates and said, with her round glasses misting up, 'I'm afraid Miss Harvey has gone.'

I solemnly handed over the pussy willows. 'Will you give her these when she gets back. I picked them myself.'

JANE LAPOTAIRE

It is only with hindsight that I realise I grew up in an urban environment. Ipswich was not then, in the late Forties and early Fifties, the built-up commuter town it has since become. It was Wolsey's Ipswich. Or rather we schoolgirls were taught that the Cardinal was its greatest claim to fame. But we knew it as a town dominated by the fields of sugar beet and wheat that surrounded it, presided over by Ransomes, Sims and Jeffries who made the agricultural machinery that safely gathered it all in. Seeing the brightly coloured ploughs and combine harvesters trundling along the Nacton Road on lorries from the factory to the fields was proof enough that we did, in fact, live in the country. And who was to deny it? Open fields and Nacton Shores were only a two-mile bike ride away. That was where my foster mother, my foster sisters and I went 'winkling', or at least that was the excuse we made to escape the back yards with their Anderson shelters.

I never actually saw anyone eat winkles. My foster mother was very partial to an occasional plate of whelks and I thought it fun to extract the rubbery inner tubes with a needle and plop the gristly, grey remains into a dish of vinegar ready for her to eat, but I had never seen anyone eat the smaller version.

The tide was *always* out when we reached Nacton Shores, having cycled through lanes overhung with beech, silver birch and elm, and the nearest we ever got to the winkles was their sharp shell edges scratching our legs as we waded, forbidden, through the miles of oozing mud.

What a blessing our bikes were – our passports to freedom. Even mine, with its shaming curved crossbar and rickety front basket attached with non-matching straps. Off we'd go to Rushmere Heath, acres of prickly broom, awash with red admirals and cabbage whites that we'd try to catch in jam jars. Earlier in the year, the jam jars would be home to jellied frog spawn, fascinating in its early stages. But once the tadpoles had grown legs and threatened to escape their glassy prison they were altogether more daunting.

My memory hasn't improved the summers. Recollections of outings to Felixstowe are coloured by the biting wind that whipped across the churning grey water, stinging legs with its chilly teeth and making shirred elastic swimming costumes stick to shivering bodies with determination, as we hopped from one frozen foot to the other.

The crossroads at Snape were known to us as the best fish and chip shop place in the whole of our Suffolk world, and not as a landmark for the Aldeburgh Festival. Further on, we pretended we could hear the bells of the sunken village church at

Dunwich, blown by the bracing gusts across the dunes and the coarse sea grass. No Sizewell B then.

Summer was shrimps from 'the Harry shrimp man', who rang a hand-bell to herald the arrival of his large tradesman's bike and its even larger basket of small, pink, whiskered creatures from Harwich, which he'd pour from a pint pewter mug into a brown paper bag until it was full to overflowing. We'd visit Woodbridge with its windmill of pristine white weatherboarding where we'd watch the boats bobbing together on the incoming tide; and Clare, Sudbury, Lavenham and East Bergholt, picture-postcard villages of thatch and Suffolk pink-wash. The Dedham tea-rooms were way beyond our pockets, so after rowing on the river – not much changed since Constable's time – we'd happily make do with potted-meat sandwiches or meat pies from Jacksons' pie shop, wrapped in crackling, grey, greaseproof paper.

Aunt Lizzie, who like all the very best aunts wasn't an aunt at all, lived in a farm cottage at Mendlesham and baked mouth-watering lemon curd tarts. I would walk cautiously round the nearby farmyard eyeing the cows suspiciously, but feeling

113

brave enough to throw the strutting hens a handful of grain. The Suffolk Punches with their sturdy, strong, feathered legs held me most in awe. 'Don't you go near them drays, they'll knock you inter the middle o' next week,' rang in my ears, and for once I heeded the warning.

The best summer holiday of all was spent in the farflung reaches of Beccles. Of course we didn't have a car. There were only two cars in our street, an imposing grey Mayflower and a Morris shooting brake resplendent with wood panelling, so we travelled by trolley bus or steam tram. Then there was the delight of letting down the leather strap and sticking my head out into the rushing air and clouds of steam, so that my breath was snatched from me.

In Beccles 'Uncle' John had an allotment near the river and would push me to it, seated in the glove of his wheel-barrow. Coming back, it was loaded with runner beans, fat shiny blackcurrants, yellow gooseberries bursting at their hairy seams and large leaves of dark green spinach, a hitherto untasted delight that 'Auntie' Nell would bake into a delicious concoction called, unsurprisingly, spinach pie. 'Uncle'

John would sit, sucking on his pipe, and point out the birds from the Broads that had been lured in by the fresh-turned earth, never remembering the names of any. I was too busy being mesmerised by the tubes of smoke that extended from his nostrils and the circle of smoke that hovered, unmoving, just beyond his pouting mouth.

Sunday School outings meant picnics in meadows deep in rose bay willowherb, vetch and cowslips, where dock leaves would be rubbed on nettle stings, staining white ankle socks green. Where we thought cuckoo-spit really was, and heard wood pigeons and mistook them for cuckoos. Where we hunted tirelessly for four-leaved clovers and never found a single one. Where the days were full of hide-and-seek and Corona fizzy pop. Where we thought that the time for seeking birds' nests in the hedgerows and blowing squawking noises through blades of grass would go on for ever, but which always ended too soon.

My foster mother's grandfather had been a miller in Wickham Market, though I never saw her bake a loaf of bread. But we did make our own pickled onions, and she herself would boil the ham or beetroots. The apples in the turnovers were Bramleys from local orchards, and the swedes and turnips came fresh from the market in the Corn Exchange, now a cinema and arts complex, I hear. That, I suppose, is the vital difference between now and then. Then, the country encroached upon the town; now, sadly, it is the other way round.

LAURIE LEE

As Gloucestershire boys, the games and rituals we played seemed to run through the natural order of the seasons. Most games we played for our amusement only; rituals were traditional and sometimes earned us pocket money. At the start of the year we had 'first footing' – crossing a neighbour's threshold early in the morning and wishing them 'Good Luck and a Happy New Year!' It was always best if you were the first to call; even better if you had black hair. A 'dark stranger', for some reason, was considered to be a symbol of good fortune; those of us with fair hair carried a lump of coal.

With the New Year past came the time of inexhaustible pleasures with the wintry landscapes wrapped up in snow and ice. The generosity of snow always seemed unbounded – you could eat it, drink it, throw it about, make caves or tunnels in it, cut it into slabs, build steps or walls or houses. Country snow seemed always clean and white as paper, so that you could read things in it, track birds, badgers or even foxes, and the big hob-nailed boots of your friends. As long as the hard winter lasted, our games were many – playing the xylophone on icicles hanging from the roofs, or licking the same like lollipops; and best of all, if the ice was strong enough, working up a slide across the village pond which, when perfectly polished, was a magic carpet that bore us in an effortless dream through the landscape.

Next, while the frosts still held and the roads were not yet turned to mud, came the time for whipping tops up and down the village – wooden rainbow tops, painted in bright reds and greens. The whips were simple lengths of string or long strips of leather stolen from out sisters' tall lace-up boots. The top was set in the dust, its point screwed in the ground, then whipped sharply so that it flew high through the air. If whipped properly it would settle and spin like a hummingbird rocking and quivering gently. To keep it alive you ran and whipped it again, and then it would rise singing, and spin even faster, and might strike sparks from the stony road when it landed. On the other hand, it could also sky through a window, or get caught in the whiplash and snap back and give you a bonk on the head.

Later, before the general thaw began, came the time for the bowling of hoops; and these made sparks too when driven along the road, because our hoops were made of iron. I am talking of the days when our roads weren't tarred but were surfaced with little stones and flints. Our iron hoops could strike up brilliant streams of sparks if sent at the proper angles across the stones. They could also be instruments of danger if they got out of control, and could cut open the knee to the bone. But we boys thought no less of them for that and were proud of them for their speed and power. The girls, on the other hand, were only allowed light hoops of cane, which we boys, of course, thought sissy.

Many of our games were played in the middle of the roads, which, since there was no traffic in those days – except for an occasional horse and cart, or an old man with a wheelbarrow – were considered a perfectly safe place to be. Here, squatting on our knees in a circle, we played 'knuckle-bones' or 'five-stones', a game older than Shakespeare, a game of manual dexterity, almost a feat of juggling, fiercely competitive and with many extended variations.

Traditional 'knuckle-bones' was played with the knuckles of pigs' feet, but as we, for the most part, were too poor to eat meat, we played with little stones instead. The game consisted of tossing the stones in the air, catching them on the back of the hand, manipulating some on the ground while still keeping at least one in the air, grabbing, scrapping and catching until the game was over. The mysteries of 'knuckle-bones' are too complex to explain fully, unless you happened to be born into them. They require a nimbleness, a sleight-of-hand sufficient to dazzle the eye; and the girls – it must be admitted – were better at it than we were. (But so they were at hopscotch – a game older than the Pyramids.)

Summer games were slower but no less various than others – snail-racing, an indolent pastime; 'french-cricket', played along pathways using legs as stumps; warfare with grass seeds catapulted from the bent looped stem; fishing for tiddlers; and 'fox-and-hounds' in the moonlight.

Then with each autumn came 'conkers' – a classic battle of determination and nerve – with the shiny brown chestnuts hanging on strings and then brutally bashed against each other in turn. Four things could happen in this encounter. Either the striker missed his opponent altogether, or the strings got entangled and caused an awkward pause, or both conkers colliding smashed each other to pieces, or one or other of them emerged victorious. The veteran survivor of many battles took on the value of the conkers he'd vanquished, so that you'd get a 'two-er', a 'twelve-er', even a 'forty-er', according to your various successes. I saw a 'fifty-er' once, a sharp-edged little nut looking grey and hard as a stone. I thought it to be deathless or an invincible destroyer – but some said it had been baked in an oven.

In autumn, too, was the time when we made bows and arrows – perhaps a tribute to the hunting season. Our bows were made of light springy willow, and our arrows cut from a hazel bush, straight peeled and sharpened at the end. If properly strung and used with average skill it was astonishing how powerful these bows and arrows could be, light and far-ranging as those of Persian cavalry or the mounted warriors of the Tartars. At the day's end, I remember, we'd often stand in the blue gloom of the valley and shoot an arrow vertically into the sky, and watch it climb, climb, till it caught the light of the setting sun, and hang there for a moment, gold and illuminated, before turning to plunge back into the evening's shadow. I always think that slender arrow, hanging in the sun's last glow, was the magic symbol of the Fall of the year. Then winter and Christmas would be on us once more, with snowballing and carol-singing, skating and wassailing, and the returning cycle of the seasons, with its ritual games, would begin all over again.

JOANNA LUMLEY

The first time I saw England was from the deck of a troopship, when I was eight years old. I had dreamed of England as being fields and apple trees, hills and valleys, and was shattered at how ghastly Southampton harbour was.

121

My mother, my sister and I were returning from Malaysia – or Malaya as it was then. My father, who was a Gurkha major, had remained there. We caught a train to Ashford in Kent, where we were met by Aunt Joan Mary who drove us to her pig farm at Woodchurch. I remember getting out of the car and standing there in the countryside; the scent of roses and the sound of woodpigeons and a cuckoo. That is my most lasting memory. It was completely, utterly different and yet I felt a sense of coming home.

We rented an oast house nearby at Belgar Farm which belonged to friends called the Shaws. One of my first impressions was of seeing a pear tree in full blossom and the extraordinary lushness of the English countryside. I quickly became passionately in love with the soft greens of England – with the roses in the hedges, the infinite variety of leaves, their patterns one on top of the other in the ditches, the shadowy kind of woods. In Malaya everything was green all the time, so I found it unbearably exciting to come to a country where there were bare, stark winter trees and ploughed fields which in only six months' time would be green and bursting with birds and song.

My sister and I were sent to boarding school near Hastings in Sussex but every holiday was spent at Belgar Farm. The Shaws had three ponies: Quinny, Squirrel and Brownface. All those names and faces are burned into my mind like actual people and I sported a horseshoe-shaped bruise on my leg from one of Quinny's kicks like a wound of war. Riding the Shaws' ponies was the greatest joy in the world. I was pony-mad: I used to dream about ponies, draw ponies on everything I had, long to own a pony, and gallop about like a pony when I couldn't ride one.

My aunt's farm had quite a different feeling from the Shaws'. She grew potatoes and swedes and kept pigs that were named after field marshals and generals: Claude Auchinleck and Archibald Wavell. She was running this phenomenal enterprise single-handedly and all the children helped: we were paid sixpence a day for planting or picking potatoes.

We used to go for walks every day. My mother was a great one for knowing things. She knew, and still knows, all the birds by their flight, their song, their appearance, and she taught us the names, the rhythms and the rules of the countryside. I find it sad now that people hear a bird singing and don't know or care what it is, which is why I support the work of Farms for City Children. For children who have never been in the country, feeding a small creature or collecting eggs warm from a nest full of straw is terribly exciting. You feel blessed. Being connected with animals has the most extraordinary, soothing effect.

The smell of English gardens is the most potent thing, too. The strange blue smell of hyacinths brings back the memory of my first headmistress's study – Miss Bentley's always had hyacinths in it. I was terrified – still so homesick for the Far East and my father. Every week he wrote to my sister and me and eventually he left the army because he hated being without us.

I was always cold as a child. I remember the coldness of the English summer when you are supposed to have taken off your cardigan and what you needed was an overcoat: English summer goosepimples. I remember a whole bunch of us going down to Jury's Gap near Camber Sands wearing those seersucker bathing dresses which tied around your neck, and having to go into that arctic grey sea when, in the tropics, I had swum in limpid, boiling water. We rushed into the sucking, roaring waves and afterwards staggered up the shingle beach on little bony feet to eat Marmite sandwiches and dry our hair.

Childhood memories are terribly sharp: nothing can stun you in the same way ever again. One of my sharpest is of a winter morning at Belgar Farm when I broke the ice in a ditch. Underneath, I could hear the water running on by and I felt completely safe. It was the first time I knew everything would go on and I would be part of it, that nature is indifferent to us in the kindest way. If ever I taste ice – that peculiar metallic taste – I remember that moment and that feeling. You are very lucky if you feel a connection with the natural world.

TREVOR McDONALD

There is a recurring problem in writing about one's childhood. It's the tendency to romanticise, to remember only the good parts and to gloss over or to forget the unpleasant. That's partly as it should be.

One of the most important elements in our lives is the ability to forget, and if, like mine, your childhood was spent in the warmth of the Caribbean, painting glorious pictures of times past is not at all difficult. It's as easy and as pleasant as most of the living was.

My most enduring memories of growing up in Trinidad are of what it meant to live in a small village community. There were probably no more than 20 or 30 families, about a hundred people all told. We were constantly visiting each other's houses. Children went to the same school and always played together. We were very close in every way.

The pervading spirit was a caring one. People looked out for one another and were concerned about the welfare of their fellows. Help came easily. It was part of the ethic of the group, part of the basic character of our tightly knit community.

But this came at a price. Because all members of the village community would look after children in need or in trouble, we were expected to express our gratitude by what West Indians still refer to even now as 'showing respect'. Children deferred to their elders. If we did, our young lives were prized beyond expression. West Indians of my parents' generation were incredibly devoted to the welfare of their children. They planned their careers and worked assiduously to see them achieved.

My parents began to lose me when I went to college; then when I left them again to work as a trainee journalist in the capital of Trinidad, Port of Spain; and then, most profoundly perhaps, when I left Trinidad to come to live and work in England in 1969. For me it was the start of a fresh adventure, a new challenge, a new beginning. Deep down it must have been painful for my parents. Yet it was a direct consequence of what they had so selflessly done. They had set me on a course that would lead to me leaving the community in which I was born and in which I grew up.

I was the oldest of our family of four children, two boys and two girls, and it was my responsibility to look after them. In turn, they were supposed to respect what I said. It was a system that worked with very few serious lapses.

We young boys and girls railed against the strictures imposed by the plans our parents had for us, but we could never defeat them. We fell into line because something told us our parents were right, that they knew best and were working in our interests.

Many consequences flowed from this. In my case, one of them was that I never really enjoyed school. It was all too serious. There was no margin for error or failure. Success was much too important. The drive to succeed began in primary school. My best subjects were English and Latin, and I have maintained an interest in them to this day. The classes were small, 20 or 25 at most. But from the earliest stage of my education we were put in streams, the fastest for scholarship students. My father, short of money and generally anxious about our success anyway, went to the school personally to make sure I was in line for a scholarship. I got into the class, one of only four select students, but I failed to win a scholarship. Only a hundred were offered and I seem to remember there were 3,000 or 4,000 pupils fighting for those places.

We played games – soccer and cricket mainly – and enjoyed most of all those rare excursions to support the school team in faraway towns and villages. We cleared our own pitches over many days, made bats from coconut trees and saved our pocket money to buy footballs or cricket balls. On those occasions we pretended to forget the rigours of the classroom. Holidays were never a great problem for us. School vacations were spent at home. Why would one choose to spend two weeks at a beach house somewhere in the country, when the sea was never very far away from where we lived and when we could swim in rivers and streams nearby? It was a joy just to have time away from school, in climate where, for the most part, the sun always shone, and to savour the outdoor life. It made our personalities more open, more expansive. Communication was easy. Entertainment was part of our daily lives. In some respects it all seemed a great long holiday, notwithstanding the knowledge that our parents' concern that we should all do well in our lives could at times be almost painful.

For a long time my passion was fishing. The rivers (tiny streams compared with some of the world's waterways) were replete with lobsters and bream. I would spend hours on end talking to my schoolfriends, eating sandwiches and catching fish. My glorious memories are of my father joining us. He knew everything there was to know about coaxing fish out of the river and was a kindly and generous instructor. He was a fund of stories, too, and kept us all amused. We had another reason for enjoying his company: it was wonderful to see him relax. So much of his life was spent working in our interests, for our education and for the betterment of our lives. Fishing in the company of my father is by far the most precious memory of my childhood.

We made our own fun and had all varieties of sporting competitions among teams in our area, but we enjoyed the company of our parents and other members of our extended families: grandmothers, aunts and uncles and what seemed at times to be an endless procession of cousins. The older members told us fascinating stories of what we children liked to call 'the old days'.

Ours were golden days, full of sport and fun and spiced by the affection of our parents. And we never gave a single thought to the weather. As I said before, you tend to remember the good times. I haven't forgotten the universal anxieties of growing up and getting on to make something of oneself. But what a wonderful time we had!

HILARY MANTEL

Sister Marie had a face like crumpled paper, a voice like a small donkey braying. When we were nine and at her mercy, she read out a lengthy essay called, 'The Town Child and the Country Child'. Ninety per cent of it was above our heads, but the gist seemed to be that the Town Child was sharper – street-wise, as we'd say now – while the Country Child was Richer in Those Things That Matter.

'Now,' said Sister, 'you will write a composition called The Town Child and the Country Child.'

Forty blank stony faces stared back.

I was born in Derbyshire, in what you might call an industrial village: mill chimneys, steep and winding streets, rows of blackened stone two-up-two-down houses. The sparrows were dingy, and chirped in a Manchester accent; pigeons like gang-bosses swaggered in the streets.

Yet if you raised your eyes – people seldom did, on principle – you saw the vast moorland and a wild sky. The Peak District lay to the south, Saddleworth's sinister moors to the north. Looking now at the map and moving east, I see some fifteen miles of blank space between my village and the splendidly-named Wigtwizzle. To say 'fifteen miles' gives no idea of the stripped, dangerous bleakness of the space. No wonder the villagers ignored the moorland, six days a week. They visited it on Sundays, after 11 o'clock mass.

Admission was gained by a rusty iron turnstile, leading to a stony and grassy path at the top of the village. Women would trip along in white high-heels, ready to beat a retreat. 'On the reservoirs' the path was called. To the left lay shimmering steel sheets of water. Bristling ranks of conifers were aligned like troops in battle. This was the country, after a fashion – useful, not decorative, feeding the giant maw of British industry with wood and water. Sometimes, on hot summer days, the adults led long marches; lifted me over stiles, and paused indulgently while I trailed my fishing net in brown, busy brooks.

The child's daily route was smaller, very narrow. The road home from school was winding and grey, dusty hedgerows one side and a wall on the other. When we felt particularly delighted with life, we would skip on to the path behind the wall, and negotiate our way over tussocky grass, in sight of the canning factory. It was called 'coming through the Fields'. You never told your parents. There was a whiff of the lawless about it.

And yet, we did have a park. A manicured acre or two – benches, orderly flowerbeds – but the upper slopes merged into rough grass and woodland. It was as if aldermen lived at one end, anarchists at the other.

We moved house, towards the top of the village. A long garden ran into 'Rough Fields'. Fly-bitten cows with lustrous eyes gazed at our potato patch. Our new car took us down into Derbyshire, to see 'The Wonders of the Peak'. They tired me and made me cold: the rocky defiles, the limestone outcrops, the gaping caverns where bandits had sheltered. This could not be the country. I had seen the country in a picture-book. There were cottages of honey-coloured stone. There were hollyhocks.

When I was eleven years old we moved again, to a small, discreetly prosperous Cheshire town with apple trees, cherry blossom and conversational magpies strutting on striped lawns. I read the *Observer Book of Birds,* a manual of etiquette for avians, and strolled, binoculars in hand, to see if theory and practice were in accord. Those were innocent days, in the mid-Sixties; no one thought the magpies a sporting target. And birds behaved well under the licensed, golden, middle-class sun. Starlings preened themselves in bird-baths, vaunting like peacocks, imitating blackbird and thrush. Now they imitate car alarms.

I am still unsure what the country is, and how to find it. I have a little house in Norfolk. At 5am huge machines thunder past the window, ready to mince the subsidised fields. They hardly wake me from a dream. I have never learned to see the country. I have to be instructed in it, or have it demonstrated. My grandfather stacked his hands one above the other, saying, 'It goes like this – and singing.' And when I was twelve, forewarned and mentally prepared, I did indeed see a skylark, climbing the vast steps of the air.

SARAH MILES

I was born and bred in the countryside, near Ingatestone in Essex. I don't recommend being the third child, the first girl with two older brothers and just over a year between each of you. The boys did their boyish things in the playroom, building amazingly intricate Meccano bits and bobs. These constructions should have been impressive. After all, Father was an architect, building steel works all over the world, so the designing knack was inbred. I wouldn't want to take away from the boys' brilliance, but for me it was inconceivable that they should be indoors when there were so many adventures to be had outside.

My home was the stableyard, fields, lanes, woods and bridle paths. My life centred around my pony Mischief, my ducks, hens, bantams and cockerels. I'd given all of them names, and was forever bemused by their different characters. Father was insistent that I become his goose-girl, so he bought eight huge, white, devilishly cantankerous geese, all of whom made my life a trifle tricky. They'd line up, a battalion of vicious hissing monsters, ready to peck me to death at every opportunity. Although they often seemed likely to succeed in this, they were unable to dampen my enthusiasm. What a wonderful privilege it was to be free! I was free from the moment school ended until the gong called me in for dinner, and all day in the holidays.

My mother and I weren't the best of friends in the beginning because she wasn't able to mould me into her idea of what her little 'Pusscat' (my nickname) should be. I loathed all parties and also the upper classes, preferring to spend my time with the animals, feathered creatures, the gipsies up the road, Nel at the apple farm or Margery, the cowhand's daughter.

Mother couldn't cope with my naughtiness (breaking the handle of her silver hairbrush with over-zealous spankings in the process) and finally became resigned to it: eventually she gave up on me altogether. For this surrender on Mother's part I was eternally grateful.

As long as I was home I was happy. I cannot remember ever being lonely, bored or sad. I had woven a world of so many rich textures for myself down in the stableyard that no amount of hairbrush spanking would break through to my own sweet fairyland.

My father was my hero, always dapper in his cream army breeches, cravat, brown polished cavalry boots and old tweed hacking jacket. Riding out with Father made me feel so grown up. The best times for me were when the two of us used to gallop through the bridle paths, with Father splattering me with twigs and mud as I tried desperately to keep up.

When we finally emerged from the woods there would always be a moment's difficulty in adjusting our eyes to the blinding light of Mill Green Common. There we'd tether our mounts to the rail outside the one dilapidated shop, run by Kate Camps, and I'd wait while Daddy went in to buy Crunchie bars. Sitting there on the common, listening to the distant sound of church bells and the horses munching grass in unison with our chewing, how I longed for time to stop.

When I was about seven a great pink pig called Charlie arrived, and I fell for him in a big way. At night I used to take a torch, steal a few apples, creep out and head straight for

Charlie's stable. His smell was sweet as hazel nuts, his tummy as soft as marshmallows and his green eyes twinkled at me almost as wickedly as Father's. Charlie's entrance into my life couldn't have been better timed because I had only recently lost my dog, Micky. (He had jumped through the greenhouse glass to greet me, smashing his front legs to smithereens.)

One day I came home from school longing to give Charlie a cuddle and feed my feathered gang. I changed out of my uniform quickly and rushed to the stableyard. I loved feeding all my friends: it was a responsibility of which I was extremely proud.

There was an ominous silence when I arrived. What was up, I wondered? Where were all my chickens, cockerels and ducks? The only sign of life was the hissing of the beastly geese. I made my way to my friends' playpens and found a gruesomely gory battlefield of a scene. Gizzards oozed in pools of scarlet mixed with yellow. I never knew what all the yellow goo was that dribbled over twisted necks and petrified heads.

Even unattached from their bodies I could recognise the heads: Loo, Guss, Danny. All of them had had particular characters, all of them had been different in their relationship to me. I didn't bother to keep my stiff upper lip – after all there was no one around to watch me. So I vomited up the horrors that confronted me without holding back, retching until there was nothing left to throw up. This was painful, so I took my mind off the pain by attempting the difficult puzzle of replacing each head to the correct body.

The worst moment was putting the head back on my best friend, Berty. Berty had been around before I was born. He was my rainbow cock. I loved Berty above all things and it wasn't unrequited. Berty would always be at my side, swaggering about, fluttering his rainbow feathers at me while I was grooming Mischief as if to say: 'Take a look at these feathers today, Pusscat!'

Finally Daddy arrived amid the bloody remains. He found me weeping as I cradled Berty's head in my arms, gently rocking him to and fro. As he opened his arms to me my floodgates opened, too, and there was no stopping me.

'Never mind, Pusscat,' he said. 'We still have all eight geese.'

I ached for retribution. I got it, too – and how. I had the means to avenge that loathsome fox's work. I began fox hunting in earnest.

JOHN NETTLES

It is the clay I remember, clay everywhere. Clinging to the pillion of my father's antique, fork-sprung motorbike as we hammered to the top of windy Penpillack Hill, I could see, dancing through my tears, the massive pyramids of clay waste ranged against the setting sun. From St Austell to the far Indian Queens the clay was everywhere. Blasted and washed from the walls of the great opencast mines at the base of the tips, it was turned into slurry and fed into the 'dries'. There, it was transformed into powder so fine that a stone might sink in it, then shipped through the ports of Fowey and Charlestown to the unknown outside world.

Much was left behind. The leaves of the trees and bushes, even blades of grass, were hung about with a white film, like an eternal hoar frost; the roads were white with clay fallen from the convoys of lorries roaring from the dries to the ports. The rivers and streams ran milky white with clay, and turned the sea in St Austell Bay to an exquisite turquoise much admired by tourists who took it to be God's handiwork. The Cornish were not about to disabuse them. A thick floor of clay lay across the bed of the sea and when we waded in the water in our woolly trunks, the white mud would squeeze up between our toes and make us laugh. It was a place like no other, and this was my childhood home.

Many of my friends had fathers who worked the clay. They seemed remote and a little frightening to me. Their skins were white through lack of sunlight and their eyes raw, red-rimmed with the dust, the clay ingrained in every pore, crease and wrinkle. They all smoked cheap cigarettes and, almost without exception, appeared to suffer some unforgiving illness that sapped their powers of speech and movement. Many died years before their time because of cancers and chronic chest complaints. They were always distantly kind to me and, as was only right and proper, I was distantly respectful to them – these men who knew the secrets of the clay mine, linhay and dry where I had never been.

St Austell was not a rich community by any means. I remember one boy crying from

141

sheer cold one dark winter because his clothes were little more than rags. I remember, too, his father arriving at school straight from work, covered in clay, false teeth discarded, and remonstrating in dignified fashion with a teacher who had singled out his son in front of the whole school for being so badly dressed.

I cared little at the time for such things, monstrous though I later understood them to be, because I was in love with Barbara Gillespie, the publican's daughter. Long blonde hair, pale blue eyes, winning smile – she was the mistress of my soul. The problem wasn't so much how to win her as how to get her to notice me at all. The time to make contact had to be the music and movement class when the teacher, Miss Coombs, sorted us into boy-girl parts. I could not hope to win her as my rich friend, Ben Lyon, might, with promises of penny ice lollies from Arnold's little shop at lunch time. I could not hope to compete with Peter Cox as far as looks were concerned. I would have to rely on wit and charm.

On the morning of the class I scrubbed hard at my face and combed my hair with my father's Brylcreem. Glowing with cleanliness, hair gleaming and wearing a new Aertex shirt, I set out for school accompanied by my mother and her sister Aunty Bertha. We went down the steep hill from the terrace above St Blazey where we lived. At the bottom of the hill we encountered a herd of cows heading up the hill to their pasture. My head full of amorous ambitions, I slipped on a cow-pat. My mother rushed me back to our little house and performed some hasty restoration work. I was late for school.

Music and movement had already begun and Cox was sitting next to the wondrous Barbara and trying to wheedle his way into her affections. I went straight up and sat on her other side and tried to engage her in conversation. She enquired gracefully enough why my shirt and trousers were wet and my shoes caked. I gave a heroic account of my dangerous encounter with unyielding nature. Her response was extraordinary. Instead of sympathy and perhaps a gentle squeezing of my hand, she held her nose, emitted strange whooping sounds and leapt off to the other side of the room. Further humiliation followed. Miss Coombs chose Cox and my Barbara to lead the dancing. Because there were more boys than girls I had to dance with Freddy Jones, noted only for his perpetually running nose.

In despair, I looked up my old friend Phyllis Banbury. She may not have been pretty, but she lived on a farm and had a proper gang and tore her skirt along the seams so she could run faster and bit chunks out of loaves of bread and swore to her mother it was the mice and did not mind farming smells one little bit! So away I ran and forgot, at least briefly, about Peter Cox and perfidious Barbara.

The incident passed and, in truth, hardly disturbed the huge enjoyment I had in life. Peter is dead now, gone with the clay tips, the milky rivers and the turquoise sea. We used to think then there was 'no more behind but such a day tomorrow as today, and to be boy eternal!' I hope he enjoyed his childhood as much as I did.

NIGEL NICOLSON

I was terribly spoiled as a child. Until I was twelve I lived in a lovely old house called Long Barn in the Weald of Kent, and then at Sissinghurst Castle, also in the Weald. But that wasn't all. My grandfather was the owner of Knole, only two miles from Long Barn, outside Sevenoaks. It was the largest private house in England (it is now a property of the National Trust, like Sissing-hurst), and we had our own permanent rooms there, which wasn't difficult for there were said to be 365 of them, though no one has ever been able to count them accurately.

Knole was a wonderful place in which to grow up. We always spent our Christmas holidays there, and a month in summer. The house is surrounded by a great park teeming with beautiful deer, and my brother and I had the freedom of it with our bikes and ponies. Our friends were the children of the estate workers, and through them we met the woodmen, the carpenters, the sawyers, the plumbers, the mechanics, the night-watchman – for Knole was then almost self-sufficient and very feudal. There was even a man whose only duty was to wind up the innumerable clocks. When it rained the huge house was our playground, with its many staircases leading to attics as long and high as galleries, and staterooms where we wandered at our peril because the contents were so valuable and fragile.

Long Barn was a great deal simpler. My

parents owned a small farm near the house, let to a sturdy woman called Vera, and she would show us how sheep were sheared, hops grown, cows milked. My mother Vita Sackville-West would often come with us, for she was then composing her long poem *The Land*, and needed to refresh her memory of farming skills. I would like to claim, as she did in the opening lines of that poem, that 'the country habit had me by the heart', but my brother and I remained surprisingly ignorant of the life that simmered all around us. I never saw a calf born until I watched it on *All Creatures Great and Small*. I now wish that I had shown more energy and curiosity. It was always remembered against me that I once asked my mother: 'mummy, have I had tea?' She must have despaired of her sons, she who loved the country so profoundly.

But there was butterfly chasing. This I was introduced to by Virginia Woolf, my mother's most intimate friend at that time, and she often stayed at Long Barn. In her own childhood she had collected butterflies and moths voraciously, and there were many more of them then than now: clouds of painted ladies, brimstones, commas, red admirals. She would call to me, 'Come on, into the fields!' and we strode with our nets through the long grass into the glades of oak and beech. I think we released almost all the butterflies that we caught, but it was the delight of spotting a rarity that made these expeditions so delightful, for she knew them all.

Once she paused, leaning on her long bamboo-handled net like a native on his assegai, and then said to me: 'What's it like to be a child?' I replied: 'You know what it's like, Virginia, because you've been one. I don't know what it's like to be you, because I've never been grown-up.' Afterwards she said to my mother: 'That boy must become a politician. He knows how to avoid answering questions.' But we adored her.

When we moved to Sissinghurst in 1930, life was even more rural than it had been at Long Barn. Indeed it was primitive. For the first few years we drew our water from a well, and ate by candlelight. My task was to help clear the future garden of the accumulated rubbish of centuries. My father would spend his evenings bent over a drawing-board, plotting where the paths, hedges and walls should run, and in daylight I held the ends of taut string and measuring tapes while he staked out his vistas and the flowerbeds that Vita would plant.

It was an idyllic life. Sissinghurst, too, had its own farm, but we spent less time in the fields than in the woods and beside the streams, one of which was diverted to form two small lakes, where we could swim, boat and fish. We always had dogs, usually Alsatians, and there were pigeons, budgerigars, ducks, goldfish and owls in addition to the farm animals to keep us company. Except at harvest-time, when we helped gather in the hops, we did not interfere very much with the farm.

As boys, we were more industrious indoors than out, stimulated by our parents' industry. Vita was busy scribbling bestselling novels in her tower-room to pay our school fees, while my father Harold could write as many as five articles in a weekend as well as read three books for review. Sissinghurst became a sort of family university.

But precisely because there were few other distractions, and because we had few friends of our own age, the countryside became our playground. I became, at last, a true country boy. My brother Ben never did. He was the urban son, I the rural, and that was why Vita bequeathed Sissinghurst to me, and more moveable property to Ben.

Growing up in a garden that has become one of the most famous in England was a very great privilege. But it is only a refinement of the surrounding countryside. While the garden was constantly developing and changing, the farmland still seems to be identical to that I knew as a child. The streams follow the same courses: no broader, no faster flowing. The hedges are fixed for centuries in the same alignments, and if the woodland rides have been trimmed and marginally drained by the National Trust, the great beeches that I used to climb are still climbed by my grandsons, and they, like me when I was their age, float bulrushes across the lake and stare with curiosity at the cows.

JILL PATON WALSH

My country childhood began in London, on a dismal cold night in 1940, with three air raids. My stepgrandfather was visiting us. He had come on business from the far distant St Ives in Cornwall. None of the family knew him well, as he had married my grandmother only recently. Three times that night the family all got out of bed, hastily put overcoats over nightwear, and trudged to the air-raid shelter, only to come back and clamber into rumpled and chilly beds again when the all-clear was heard. I can remember none of this; it is family legend. But it seems the next morning, Grandpa Isaac said, 'You can't live like this' and at 10.30 that morning we were all – my mother, myself, my two younger brothers, and all our possessions – on the famous train, *The Cornish Riviera*, that left Paddington for the run to Penzance.

My grandmother went down to the station in the early evening and found her entire family on the platform, come to stay for ever – or at least until after the war.

St Ives is a famously beautiful place; a town of crooked, sloping streets, a stone harbour on a wide bay, golden beaches and a lighthouse on a distant rock that can be seen from all over the town. In the war years it was not crowded with tourists, it was still busy with fishing boats and haunted by a million contented cats. A sweeping view of town, beaches and bay could be seen from every window of Gran's house, and a path to the beach led down from a gate at the foot of the garden. We seemed to have landed in heaven.

We had certainly landed in a comfortable house – there were two servants and attics for us to sleep and play in. And, which impressed us more at the time, our Cornish Grandpa could afford to buy endless sweets on the black market and give them to any children he met. I remember his defence. 'If anyone is having them, then *anyone* is having them!'

I do not know what made my mother return to London. But by the time she did I had started at a little nursery school and my grandmother argued it would be better for me not to change schools. Both my brothers, and my sister, who was born by then, went back and I was left in St Ives.

And I don't remember missing the others at all. Left with my grandmother I was spoiled, praised and made much more of in every way and went on doing well at school. My grandparents were elderly newlyweds and their happiness surrounded me like a spell of fine weather.

But the safety and the spoiling were not to last. Late in 1944 my grandmother died very suddenly of a heart attack. Lying in my bed, I heard her come to bed unusually early, and run a bath. I ran across the land-ing to hug her in the soft dressing gown and tell her about something I had been reading. 'Goodbye, darling,' she said. I laughed. 'You mean goodnight, Granny, not goodbye,' I said. 'Yes,' she said. 'Goodnight. Don't read too long.'

But I read long enough to hear people scrambling round the house and talking in agitated whispers. They were still doing it when I fell asleep. The next morning was a nightmare. The grown-ups in the house were my stepgrandfather's children. They told me Granny was in bed, too ill to see anyone. But I had slipped into her room the moment I woke to wriggle down beside her for my morning cuddle. I knew that the bed, smooth, flat and cold, had not been slept in. My head was full of *Grimm's Fairy Tales* about wicked step-relations, and church talk about the wickedness of lying, and I was frightened.

My terror lasted only as long as it took a train from London to reach the end of England. At dusk there was someone at the door. Someone told me, 'Your mother is here,' and I raced out and flung myself, weeping, into the newcomer's arms. I was blurting out between tears that Granny had gone and nobody would say … 'my God,' said my mother, 'has nobody told the child?' At which my grandfather, appearing at the top of the stairs, put the lights on, and I saw that I was holding hard to someone whose face was wet with tears. I was clinging to my mother, but I could not remember her at all.

I was back in London for the last of the bombs. Re-adjusting to the real world and family life was not easy. And so St Ives became my personal Garden of Paradise. I have often revisited it, I have written about it, and I have a flat there now. I never return without being engulfed by an extraordinary sensation of happiness. It is a radiantly beautiful place, but I think this has more to do with my grandparents' autumnal love for each other, and for the lucky, over-indulged child I was.

TOM PAULIN

I believe there are primal, original land-scapes of the imagination. Often they are the places in which we grew up and which remain important to us throughout adulthood. For me that landscape is Donegal. My parents moved from Chapel Allerton, in Leeds, to Belfast in 1953, shortly after the Coronation, when I was four. In the mid-1950s they started to take me and my two brothers on family holidays to a place on the Gweebarra Bay, known as Portnoo – that's its modern name which refers to a concrete quay the British Government put up to encourage fishing. Its Gaelic name is Narin.

It's the part of the world I am fondest of – a beautiful mountainous landscape to which I feel compelled to return again and again, even though I have lived in England since 1967 when I came over as a student. When I moved to America for a year I held on to images of Donegal: I was terrified of not being able to relate to that landscape, of becoming what Yeats called the 'world's besotted traveller'.

Eventually that fear passed. I returned to England and I have been going back to Portnoo for forty odd years – at Easter and Hallowe'en, in summer and winter. I meet friends there that I made at eight or ten years old. It's like a time warp, a way to hold on to childhood, and it's part of my sense of place. At night we reminisce about our childhood – how we used to take an old golf putter and hook edible crabs from the crevices at low tide. In the old days we used to get a sack load; now the crabs are all cleaned up by the trawlers.

There are three strands. In the summer there are lots of people on the first one, fewer on the second, and the third is deserted. In the bay there is the island of Inishkeel with a ruined liskeel (church) and monastery and when there is a spring tide you can walk to it. At Whitsun birds nest there – eider ducks, terns, oyster catchers, seagulls. As a child I remember discovering a scaldie (chick), struggling bald and blind out of its shell. In the last ten years I have taken my two sons, my nephew and niece there too. A few years ago, in the almost Mediterranean summer, we pitched a tent at the end of the island's far strand, made fires out of driftwood and fell asleep to the sound of the boom of surf.

As a teenager I used to take a boat out to watch shoals of mackerel fry seething like gravel in the still ocean. Watching the fish breaking the surface again on a recent trip, I remembered Yeats's phrase 'the mackerel crowded sea', recalling his own childhood in Sligo. I have seen dolphins and porpoises leaping there too.

My childhood summers were planned around bird-watching. One July, on Cashel Goland strand, I remember pulling back the marram grass on the sand dunes and finding four greenish eggs – it must have been a plover nest. Another year, a friend told me that he had seen the only nesting red-throated diver in Ireland. He wouldn't tell me where. Then one day my French exchange friend Patrice and I were fishing in a lock when we found two red-throated divers hidden in the water lilies. It was strange. I have always admired the way John Clare, the Nineteenth-Century Northampton-shire poet, writes the strangest, most detailed poetry about birds and their nests. I remember, too, the stony cry of the chough and the corncrake racketing away in a field in the centre of the village.

Other childhood memories revolve around afternoons spent in the one-storey cottage on the coast, which my parents had built in 1960, reading *Bulldog Drummond* stories: isolation and boredom, no television, just the consolation of a turf fire. Rural life can become a desperate parochialism. But at least Irish villages are sprawling clachans (hamlets) of undistinguished modern architecture. I find English villages hard to identify with – they are too neat, too old. And I feel alienated in the English countryside: I may have an Aga in my house in Oxford but I find the Cotswolds too tame.

I can relate to the wilder country of Yorkshire and I feel the pull of the ancient South Downs – the chalk landscape with which the London-born, First World War poet Edward Thomas struggled to identify. He, too, felt the alienation of an urban intellect.

ELLIS PETERS

My native county, Shropshire, is a region of contradictions, and the place where I was born and bred encapsulates all of them. It lies in the quite limited district where the Industrial Revolution began, and in my early years half its population worked in mining and heavy industry, though already in decline. The village – hardly large enough to be called a village – consisted of two or three short stretches of minor road, sporadically lined with small houses in semi-detached blocks or short, untidy terraces, and everything around was wholly rural. The men not employed at the ironworks or small local pits farmed, and the surrounding land was rich both for stock and arable use.

There were plenty of evidences of industry scattered about this idyllic countryside, but they were evidences 100 to 150 years old. In that time industrial pools had greened and mellowed into haunts for wildfowl, full of reeds and waterlilies, while pennystone spoilheaps had become copses of birch and heathy spaces of bramble, furze and wild roses.

I was the youngest of three, with a brother five years ahead of me, and a sister two years my senior, and we had several cousins living within comfortable reach. We three attended a Church of England school a mile distant from home and walked there and back twice a day. There were no school dinners then – home dinners were the order of the day – and we took the walking for granted. I enjoyed school and, like my siblings, had the advantage of being able to read and write before I entered at five years old. Our mother, a great reader herself and a lifelong self-educator (though she had left formal schooling behind at thirteen), taught us to read without actually teaching us. She read to us constantly, and the rest seemed to happen of itself.

We had a walk of nearly a mile to church, too. The Sunday School year, quite apart from the festival seasons of Christmas, Easter and Whitsun, was punctuated by three major events: the midsummer Egg and Flower Service, when all the children brought masses of those two commodities to the altar and then conveyed them to the local hospitals; the annual treat, open-air in the neighbouring field if the weather was fine – as almost invariably it was – with tea, games, pony rides and ice cream; and the concert in the late autumn, when we all performed action songs, sketches and dances, and showed off like mad before a captive audience of parents and patrons.

Locally the year was marked off by the seasonal games that succeeded one another in some immemorial order that had no written rules. There was a time for marbles, unhampered by dark evenings since it was played under the lamp-posts, a time for hopscotch, for hoops, for tops, for skipping ropes, for tipcat and, in the dark, for ranging games – hare and hounds over the mounds and meadows with a torch.

To favourite playgrounds we would decamp for a long half day, a mile or more distant from home. Planned adventure playgrounds are no match for ours. For cops and robbers, cowboys and Indians, knights and castles, the wide heaths grown from spoilheaps a hundred years dead, and long since taken back into abundant life, were ideal.

For more secret and mysterious goings-on, mostly concerning captive princesses, witches and magicians, and created usually by the girls, there was the deep gully of a brook going down to the Severn, with a pool and a broken bridge from old industry deep within its wooded folds. There we had brushwood huts and a complete map of a private country, where the paths and glades had their own names, and we found violets, primroses, bluebells and anemones in season. That time of my life was pre-television, almost pre-radio, or we might have spent it less richly.

We did things as a family, too, whenever the ironworks closed down for a Bank or annual holiday. We thought nothing of walking twenty miles to visit some attraction, a country house or a beauty spot. And

Sunday evenings, on all but the dark nights of winter, were spent in long country walks, all of us together. My mother was endlessly interested and curious, knew virtually every wildflower by name, if not by several names, and if we found one she did not know, would ransack the bookshelves and libraries to find out what it was.

She knew the songs of birds, too. And she loved dogs, as we all did and I still do. We had in succession Kim, who was a fighter, but fought fair, never picking on a smaller opponent; Jet, as black as his name, but a wanderer; and a terrier bitch called Tigger. Much earlier – he was one of the family before I was born – we had a beautiful old English terrier named Tory, who was so beloved that after his death there was an interval of some years before we admitted Kim into the vacancy.

We made good use of the natural bounty the country provides. At Easter we gathered gorse blossoms to dye our Easter morning eggs gold. There was a time for gathering blackberries from the bramble-covered pitmounds, mushrooms from the meadows, and crab apples for jelly from the trees growing in the hedgerows. Much of our wild domain is built over now. Ecologically I think we did it no harm in taking what it freely offered.

My sister and I took to making up stories early. We took it in turns to tell them while we helped with housework on Saturday mornings. She was far better at it than I, but she never wrote them down. I'm sure that a great deal of what I have written since owes much of its wit and spirit, if such it has, to the tales my sister tossed off so lightly over the dusting, and left to blow away with the dust.

They were good times. I wish as good to all children.

SIAN PHILLIPS

Life, in the upper reaches of the Tawe and Twrch valleys on the border of Glamorganshire and Carmarthenshire, was lived at a rolling boil, emotionally speaking. The contradictions were enough to start a child off on several lifetimes of confusion, where confidence and insecurity flourished side by side. The notion that there was nothing that we could not achieve provided we did our homework, respected the Sabbath, obeyed our parents and washed regularly, was dispensed as part of our daily diet. Coupled with urgent recommendations to us not to think that we were anything special, because we weren't and no one would be looking at us anyway. South Wales was still reeling from the Depression, the Second World War was coming to and end, we were very little and this assumption that our future might hold fame and power, let alone money, had a quixotic gallantry which was, in a real sense, disarming – there was to be no escape from realising our potential. As role models we duly adopted John James (the 'Demosthenes' of South Wales miners), Dr John Thomas and – more current – Jim Griffiths.

Whoever this Karl Marx was who featured so prominently in fireside conversations, he couldn't compete with God who was everywhere, but paying special attention to me. I longed for him to take an afternoon off so I could misbehave in peace. A hideous pictorial representation of the saved and the damned made a great impression on me. An all-seeing eye looked down on a narrow, dreary little path up which the righteous laboured towards a Pearl & Dean paradise, while the damned strolled down a broad thoroughfare, doing rather jolly things before falling into the Pit. It wasn't piety that held me in thrall; I couldn't make a final decision when life could be so wretchedly sad and unfair.

Take pig-killing time, when all over the village children sobbed noisily and mothers averted their eyes from the back yard where the family friend (and source of winter food) was being dispatched to a better place, with what sounded like a heroic fight. The misery of seeing the clean, empty sty vied against the guilty pleasure of acquiring a new place to play house. Yet our pig-killer was benign compared with the travelling slaughterer of my mother's childhood. I made her tell me over and over again how, after a whole day of butchering in one of the outhouses, he would appear in the yard holding a carcass from which he would cut a slice and eat it, saying 'sweet as a nut, Mrs Lomas, sweet as a nut,' while the family looked on in horror. He'd follow this scene by climbing on to a pile of hides, drawing one over his head, to sleep exhausted by his labours. I never learned not to make friends with farm stock. In those days cows had names and very distinct, strong personalities too. Also, I was very partial to the cake they ate and there's something about sharing food... Bouts of vegetarianism coincided with peaks of mourning when one of them shuffled off. My own pet animals were legion and courted death with their reckless behaviour; my dogs ate chickens, my parrot bit off someone's ear-lobe and my rabbits burst from over-eating. Every creature, even stick insects, had to be formally dispatched from this world. Graves had to be dug, eulogies written and delivered and crosses were nailed and poker-worked. My bit of garden was a desolate spot.

It wasn't only animals I had to worry about. My life was crammed with old people. Being an only child and making something of a career of being an invalid (this was a time when diphtheria, scarlet fever, jaundice, measles and so on could carry one off), it was regarded as enough on my part that I should be alive at all, and for long periods I was allowed to do more or less as I pleased. I had regular calling places in isolated outlying farms where they saw so few people that, I correctly supposed, any sort of visitor was welcome. Houses where I could be pretty sure of tea and a bit of a rummage through the treasures of The Parlour, which always smelt of chapel and frequently housed a harmonium or old piano and I would oblige with a little over-expressive Chopin or an unwise rush at a bit of Souza. I became devoted to elderly, sometimes ancient people. 'It seems,' my father said during one of my fits of weeping, 'to be in the nature of the goldfish to, um, die,' and I had to come to terms with the fact that the same law applied to aged people. Once I was taken into the parlour to pay my last respects to the corpse laid out for adults only to view. I was deeply sensible of the honour and very thoughtful for quite a few days.

Then there were seasonal friends – well, hardly friends; people I counted on seeing regularly. There were tramps who worked the same routes year in year out. One was a tall, well set-up, respectable looking woman. Sitting under the kitchen table until the women forgot I was there, I had learned that she had upped and left her good family, for no reason that anyone could make out, and she simply walked and walked. When she passed by I would take a short cut and join her once she was out of my mother's sight. I would walk with her for three or four miles, but never once did she speak to me. This increased her fascination.

One of my gentlemen friends was very

talkative and I thought that he was wonderfully clever. He would build a lean-to rainproof roof against a disused coal-mine that he favoured as a stopping place. We never discussed people but he told me the names of trees and let me drink tea out of a tin.

Wales is wetter than Borneo and my childhood wasn't bathed in sunshine, but there were big skies over the Black Mountains, the topsoil almost washed away and the smooth flanks reflecting fast-moving clouds. On the Gwrhyd and March Hywe the cairns and barrows of prehistory were as much a part of home as the overgrown roadways of my great grandparents' day, and everywhere, like reference points, the chapels: Soar, Bethesda, Gosen, Siloh, Carmel, Caersalem...

ROSAMUNDE PILCHER

I was born in 1924, in a boarding house called No 1 Chilecito Villas, in Lelant in Cornwall. My father had left for a job in Rangoon, Burma, and my mother, with my five-year-old sister to care for and me on the way, decided that if she was going to have to live on her own Cornwall would be a good place to bring up her children.

It was for the two of us an inspired decision. In Lelant we took possession of The Elms, a large Victorian granite-built house, and semi-detached, where we stayed until the outbreak of war. Our neighbours were the Harveys who had two boys. To begin with we all hated each other and had terrible battles, throwing rotten apples and shrieking insults as we rode to and fro on our bicycles. But they had an older cousin called Geoff, and he decided that the next-door girls weren't too bad (in particular my sister who was slender and blonde) and in the end we all became friends.

The Elms had a perfect position on a hill above the Hayle estuary, with the railway line running along the edge of the shore, headed around the cliffs towards St Ives. The station was tiny and wooden and had a first-class waiting room, a third-class waiting room, a smelly lavatory, and a machine which, on being fed a penny, dispensed Nestlé's chocolate.

The railway and the station were an important part of our lives. Sometimes we dressed up and stood on an old crossing gate to wave like maniacs at startled passengers. We slipped through the railings and crossed the tracks, because that was the quickest way to get to the estuary beach, and Charlie, the engine driver, always tooted his whistle as he came through the cutting, giving us plenty of time to scatter like pigeons.

In summer we all went down to the big beach, which entailed walking through the village, past the church and over the golf course. Most people foregathered at the church and a little cavalcade of children, nannies, pushchairs, dogs and sometimes a gallant parent or two would make its way over the scented links to the dunes and the huge empty sands.

Lelant was a dangerous beach. We knew not to swim on the ebb tide, and would play in the dunes or construct waterworks until the tide turned, someone gave a shout, and we all galloped out across the miles of beach to fling ourselves into the shallow breakers.

Each family brought their own tea picnic, and it was at that time that I learned that great truth: other people's picnics are always infinitely better than one's own.

Sometimes we caught the train to St Ives and swam on Porthminster beach, which had the added attraction of tents, sun umbrellas and ice-cream huts. As well, summer was the time when friends and relations came to stay. Our favourite visitors were the Gilberts, old colleagues from Burma, who brought with them four lively daughters, a canary in a cage, an old spaniel and two capacious motor cars. As we didn't own a car this was a tremendous treat, and we all used to pile aboard and be driven to Prussia Cove, or Rinsey or Prah Sands.

Winters could be very wild. Storms blew ships on to the rocks beyond St Ives, and the lifeboat was called out to rescue crews in trouble. Over the howl of the wind we could hear the distress rockets and the next morning the local paper would fly banner headlines of disaster and give us all the gory and sometimes tragic details.

We seldom had snow, but when we did, I hated it because it made my hands so cold. Our house had no central heating. The warmest room was the kitchen, where the Cornish range burned all day, and there was a smell of freshly ironed linen and baking.

Christmas holidays were a round of parties and plays. Not plays we went to watch, but plays we took part in. In St Ives there was the Arts Club, and some enthusiastic mother would somehow dragoon us into putting on a show. The Arts Club was an integral part of St Ives, because not only painters had settled in the little town, but potters, sculptors, poets and writers, too. My mother was, for some reason, an honorary member, although she had never created anything more ambitious than a cotton frock, but it meant that we met all the interesting inhabitants of St Ives, and more importantly, their children.

Our favourite artists were George and Kay Bradshaw. Their studio looked out over Porthmeor beach, and we used to go there for picnic teas, climb out of the window by means of a rope ladder, and ride the pounding surf on wooden belly-boards.

Another of my mother's friends was Mrs Dow, the widow of Thomas Millie Dow, the painter. Mrs Dow's eldest daughter was Mrs Griggs, who farmed Tremedda, out at Zennor on the Land's End road. Mrs Griggs had four daughters. From time to time we were asked to Tremedda for tea, where the smallest daughter, Flora, younger than myself, astounded me by her ability to milk a cow. Then, I never imagined that I should end up married to Flora's Scottish cousin, so that Mrs Dow became Granny Dow and Mrs Griggs became Aunt Elsie.

I still go back. Lelant has changed, but in winter St Ives is still as I remember it: the cobbled streets bleached by the brilliant light and the sea winds; the gulls screaming, and the surfers like seals in their glistening black wet suits, riding the breakers on Porthmeor beach.

SIR LAURENS VAN DER POST

I think you could say that my respect for nature and love of animals stem even from before my childhood. Nowadays everyone talks about genes. We must have had a special gene, particularly in my mother's family. They went to Africa in 1685 and were at the fore of the thrust into the interior. They were part of the community that was in contact with Africa as it was at the beginning – the Africa that was one of the greatest reservoirs of natural life we've ever had on earth.

I was born in the interior of southern Africa, beyond the Great River – the Orange

River – nearly 1,200 miles from the sea. I was the thirteenth of fifteen children, born on 13 December. Had there been a thirteenth month I would have been born in that, I am certain.

By the time I was born my father, who was a statesman and a distinguished person in South African public life, had retired to be in the country, to live on our farms. Most of the farms had come from my grandfather's pioneering efforts. Together they made quite an empire.

From the very earliest I was in constant contact with the natural world. I had the most vivid impressions of animals. The farms were really great game parks: we still had springbok and other antelopes, and leopards and lynxes and jackals and hyenas, and tremendous bird life. I never went out in the morning on to the stoep – the raised terrace of the house – without seeing animals in the distance all around us.

My first memory of a human being is of Klara, my nurse. She had a shining blue necklace which caught the sunlight, and a wonderful face, the face of the ancient Bushmen. I remember her always with extraordinary emotion; we were very close. I was nine when she died.

It was Klara who talked to me about her vanished people, about their legends and customs, about their interpretations of the natural world. It was Klara who taught me that if necessary I could survive in the wild. The women in Bushmen life were the botanists and the food-gatherers, and I am certain that if ever, even as a boy, I had been turned loose – that if civilised life had disappeared – I would have been able to keep myself alive by eating the things that Klara had taught me to find, the things that grew in the soil as well as above it.

I didn't have a favourite animal. I loved them all. Even the insects. Unlike other African peoples, the Bushmen have an enormous knowledge of insect life. Being small themselves they have a predilection for life that is small. Knowing as much about the insects as about the greater animals meant that I understood from an early age that everything on earth had an equal right to be there, that everything belonged.

As a family we camped out every year for about three weeks down by the Orange River, which ran deep at the bottom of our territory. We took covered wagons and oxen; it was like a reconstruction of the Great

Trek. We would swim and fish in the river, and in the evenings follow bees up into the cliffs, find their nests and take out their honey. We spent one of my first Chrismases there: my childhood Christmas memories are not of snow, but of the natural noises of Africa, strung like beads on a long necklace around the throat of the night.

It was the darkness that made the stars important. The moon was lovely, but I was glad when it wasn't there because the stars were so much brighter. Klara told me the Bushmen had no chiefs, no kings and no gods, and prayed to the stars instead. Some were male, others female, and they would say 'Grandmother so-and-so, may I have this?' or 'Grandfather so-and-so, may I have that?' The greatest honorific in the Bushmen language was to refer to someone as either a grandfather or a grandmother.

I once wrote that perhaps one of the greatest burdens of being a child is that one is always expected to take, and so rarely thought to be in a position of ever wanting, or needing, to give as well. People seemed either not to have experienced this when they were young, or to have been educated out of it by the time they are older and so don't honour it in their own children. The importance of giving, particularly to the land, was drummed into us by our parents more than anything else.

For me, the satisfaction of giving to nature came mostly through the giving of water. One of our duties was to irrigate the flower and vegetable gardens, guiding the waters from one plant to another. That gave me a very important sense of giving. I loved listening to the gurgling in the earth as the water seeped in, and smelling the scent that came out of it.

When I was small there was a very bad drought in South Africa. This was my first experience of lack of water. It was 1911. We got our stock through by taking food and water to them. There were thousands of them, and they became so weak they couldn't walk. Many pioneering families were ruined that year, but we were fortunate. My grandfather was a good farmer: he only ever stocked half his land; he had taught us to farm for famine, and not for the harvest.

I became obsessed at times of drought. I used to climb up on to the roof of our house at night to sit and scan the horizon for lightning, because when the rains broke the lightning always came a week or ten days before. And when it rained, a great feeling of peace came over everything. It was a wonderful feeling to go to sleep listening to the sound of the rain on the roof.

There is nothing more exciting than seeing a country which has been cruelly starved of water suddenly being given the water it needs. I call it Cinderella earth; it decorates itself like a bride, particularly in the desert where the most beautiful flowers shoot and bloom overnight. Once you have recognised nature's gratitude on that scale you can never be an ungrateful person again.

LIBBY PURVES

Tel Aviv, Bangkok, Lille, Berne, Johannesburg ... I was a diplomat's child, and foreign postings meant life in foreign lands. In some respects, it was an enviable childhood, full of images – golden Buddhas and wildebeeste, olive groves and crumbling old French courtyards. But we always lived in cities, because that is where diplomats ply their trade: except for one period, from my seventh year to my ninth, when my father was posted to one of the less healthy countries in Africa and the rest of us stayed in England. We found a house on the Suffolk coast, and it remained our base for nearly thirty years.

So I am no Laurie Lee; but my short English country childhood was enough, at that impressionable age, to make me put down immovable roots. It must have been, because three decades later, after Hamburg and Oxford and London, I seem to have ended up twenty minutes' drive from the old house, bringing up my own children among the same flat, bleak landscapes, in the same sort of draughty house, round a Rayburn coke-burning range.

And I listen to their voices starting to echo the same rising Suffolk accents, and feel very comfortable about it all. To my great pleasure, the coalman who turned up on our first day in this house was the one who used to deliver twenty-five years earlier to the house in Leverets Lane where we lived, and casually remembered that there 'used to be a pack o' little boys, and one little girl used to watch me unloading'. I felt like Rip Van Winkle, suddenly awakened to find nothing much changed after all.

There were two important things about that childhood in Walberswick: the village school and the sea. The school (now a chi-chi holiday cottage, alas) was an ugly two-roomed building in a bare concrete yard, but it was nonetheless the heart of the village. There were only two classes; until you were eight you went into the 'Little Ones', with Mrs Brown, and then progressed to the 'Big Ones', with Mrs Hargreaves. I cannot pretend that the educational standards were particularly high – at the age of nine I still believed that 'area' was where you parked aeroplanes – but we learned the basics, and above all we learned to belong.

At the desks around me were the local solicitor's son and daughter, labourers' and small shopkeepers' children, the surly offspring of the local ne'er-do-well, and the various red-headed members of an apparently limitless family from 'up the council houses'. We walked up the narrow lane together, formed alliances, fought off Alfie the bully (I once ran over his foot on my bicycle, and was a heroine for a week) and conducted intense, secret meetings after school under the gorse bushes with a supply of Wagon Wheels and bottles of Tizer. My best, best friends were Janet and Julie, and Janet's dog Gyp; I do not know where they are now, but I can't look at the old black-and-white photograph I took of them all on my mother's Box Brownie without feeling a surge of happiness and optimism, the legacy of that first, free friendship.

Because we *were* free: nobody seriously thought we little girls would be raped or murdered if we ran off in daylight down the field paths and climbed around on the warm concrete of the old wartime blockhouses and 'dragons' teeth' which litter these eastern shores. We picked ears of corn to eat, sampled mothy cabbage leaves from the edges of the field, cured our nettle stings with dock leaves and made guns out of popping-grass. We knew well enough not to swim in the sea without adults, and never to walk on to the great spits of sand by the pier unless we knew for certain sure that the tide was still falling; there had been enough drownings to convince us. We shouldn't ever talk to strangers, but there weren't many strangers except the summer tourists and weekenders; and even they were sufficiently regular in their appearance so as not to count.

In the first days of November we toured the village with a Guy on a handcart, begging wood just as earnestly as we begged money for fireworks. Once, for no very clear reason, during the summer holidays a group of us marched through the street playing the 'Z Cars' theme on motley instruments, declaring it a Parade. Nobody organised us into it, nor did it raise money: we just did it. I still don't know why; probably what Bristow would call 'devilish high spirits'.

There was a riding school which visited the village in summer, run by Major and Mrs Bugg. I had a few seven-and-sixpenny lessons and hacks, but one or twice a week was the ration (unless I collected and sold enough horse-manure off the road to pay for my own extra rides. I can hardly pass a good dollop of it, even today, without an avaricious urge to scoop it up and flog it). So Janet and I and a few other girls would get up at 6.30 am, meet at the makeshift stables, muck them out, clean tack, and then travel in Major Bugg's ancient car to the field where the ponies spent the night. The car had a rumble-seat, already in antiquity in 1959, and we fought to sit in it. There was no room for saddles, so we took bridles only and rode the ponies bareback to the village. I usually fell off, especially when I rode the Major's own horse, Timmy: it wasn't that he was an unkind animal, and he certainly wasn't a frisky one, but he was simply very wide. I didn't have enough leg to dangle down either side for balance – they stuck straight out. He got very slippery in the rain, too, so off I came into the wet heather.

But when the morning was dry and clear, and we clopped without incident across the common, I could look from my unsteady perch on his warm black back and see all the way down the River Blyth to the sea. And the gorse on the common was drying in the sunshine and smelt of summer; and my daily friends from school were riding alongside me. Paradise enough.

PRUNELLA SCALES

I was born in the bedroom of a peaceful, rented cottage in Surrey. Later, my parents took out a mortgage on a new 'Post Office Georgian' house, built just before the Second World War. But they sold it after war broke out as it was under a Luftwaffe flight-path and they were afraid it would be bombed. (Indeed, a time bomb did drop in the garden but it was defused by the local bomb disposal unit.) Our furniture went into store, my father went into the army, and we spent the war years more or less rootless.

First we stayed with my aunt, who had a small farm outside Huddersfield. My mother's family came from Bradford so I immediately loved the West Riding country-side and have remained deeply attached to it ever since. I remember the winter of 1940, when snowdrifts were more than six-foot deep, and we had to collect the groceries from the village on a sledge. We spent a lot of time out of doors, learning to bind and stook oat and barley sheaves by hand. The wheat was cut by hand, too, until one day the combine harvester arrived, which we thought tremendously modern. There was a carthorse called Jack, who was used for the ploughing. I longed to learn to ride like the children in story books – just as I longed to learn to sail, like the characters in *Swallows and Amazons* – but my parents were too hard up.

At the end of the winter of 1941, I had a bad attack of pneumonia and the doctor said I must go to the seaside to recuperate. My father was stationed in Minehead and friends told us of a cottage to rent in Bucks Mills – a village on the north Devon coast. We went for a fortnight and ended up staying two years. All the people in the village belonged to the same family, so we knew the wives by their husbands' names: Mrs Charlie, Mrs Reggie, Mrs Ernest. I remember sitting on the doorstep one day watching the village boys having a fight and howling, 'I want to be a boy, I want to be a boy,' because I wanted to join in. But Charlie came out of the cowshed with his milking buckets and said, 'Tidden proper for little maids to fight.'

We walked a mile and a quarter up the road to the village school. It was run by a Welsh woman, and the vicar, who lived in the crumbling Georgian vicarage next door, came in to teach as well. Then the evacuees arrived – about twenty of them – with their teacher, Mrs Prudence, so I learned the alphabet in cockney and the catechism in north Devon, which was very useful later as an actress.

There was a lot of bird-watching and I remember one woman living in the village whose war-time job it was to find the nests of peregrine falcons and destroy the eggs, because the mature birds would prey on War Office carrier pigeons. With the fishermen, we used to catch mackerel, which we soaked overnight in brine and ate for breakfast fried with oatmeal. And sometimes we caught prawns in the rock pools and boiled them on the beach to eat with a bottle of Heinz salad cream.

When my mother took a war-time job in her old school, which had been evacuated to Windermere, I managed to get a scholarship there and we left for the Lake District. The school was housed in an Edwardian hotel beside the lake, where we were taught to row. The hotel bedrooms became dormitories and the practice pianos were housed in the bathrooms.

We played rounders and tennis in the garden, but for lacrosse and hockey we'd go across the lake on the ferry to playing fields at Bowness. I will never forget the V-E Day celebrations with fireworks over the lake – the first we'd seen since the blackout. In the holidays we would stay in digs, sometimes Near Sawrey (which was further away than Far Sawrey). Beatrix Potter lived there, and once we saw her from the window. We were staying next door to the cottage owned by Duchess in *The Pie and the Patty-Pan*.

When the war was over, my parents returned to Surrey where they rented a tumbledown farmhouse with a fifteen-acre field for only £90 a year. We kept a couple of geese, four Khaki Campbell ducks and two hens. My brother used to shoot grey squirrels with an air gun. He got sixpence a tail from the estate office as part of the campaign to save the red squirrel. We were only about thirty-five miles from Hyde Park Corner, but there was no gas or electricity, just oil lamps and candles. My drama student friends couldn't believe their eyes when I took them there.

For my first term at drama school, I was a commuter. I walked a mile through the woods, left my gumboots at the pub, took the bus to Dorking and then a train to London. When I moved into digs in Dulwich for the second term, it really was my first taste ever of urban life.

NIGEL SLATER

My mother died when I was nine. I was devastated when my father and I moved to the country. We drove to our new home in silence on the day after I had broken up for the school holidays. He was so happy to be leaving the Black Country, and I could not bear the thought of him knowing that I didn't want to go. 'You can have a rabbit,' he said. I would rather have had my friends.

When we got there – a rambling Seventeenth-Century cottage with acres of lawns, a housekeeper, an old plum orchard, a huge goldfish pond and a kitchen garden hidden away in the depths of Worcestershire – I went to my new room and burst into tears. With red eyes and a swollen face, I told a tale about being allergic to the pollen.

As the summer wore on my father became more and more relaxed. He started to let me hug him when he came in from his greenhouse, smelling of warm potting compost and tobacco. He put on weight and took to growing tomatoes and pink and red begonias. My father and the housekeeper spent hours together in the garden, trimming the aubretia, deadheading the climbing roses and going for long walks in the woods.

A big garden is no fun if you don't have any friends to play in it. But it is a good place to hide. No one hears what you say when you talk to your new imaginary friend or sees you having fights or sharing secrets with them.

My father gave me my own patch of

garden and I planted purple Cosmos and yellow African marigolds, which stood out against his lavender bushes and Peace roses. He would explain to visitors that it was my garden and they would laugh.

Year after year my father's friends would come for Sunday lunch and go all starry-eyed just because you could see the Malvern Hills from our garden. They cooed over the perfect lawns, the honeysuckle hedges and the lambs in the fields. They went quite daft over the bluebell dell and the daffodils in the woods.

Every summer we'd go to village shows. My father would come home with cuttings for the garden, the housekeeper with pots of glorious gooseberry and raspberry jam for her mile-high Victoria sponges. I dawdled behind trying to find something horrid to tread in.

In winter there were long, frozen walks to the school bus, the snow coming in over my gumboots. Then even longer, frozen walks back when the bus didn't come.

The most exciting time was when the mobile library came and I could read another Arthur Ransome. The bread man came on Tuesdays and Fridays, bringing long white sandwich loaves and iced fancies.

The grocer drove up every Wednesday in a van that smelled of ham.

As I got older the housekeeper began to let me help her make Victoria sponges. I was allowed to cream the butter and sugar but she would do the rest. We made jam tarts with crisp, pale pastry and tiny fairy cakes with icing on top. She showed me how to salt the beans that grew up in the wigwam poles in the garden and how to freeze the strawberries she brought in from the garden in her apron. (Never, never freeze a strawberry.)

I took up domestic science at school, though my father wasn't pleased. On Wednesdays I would bring my pathetic efforts home from school in a biscuit tin to find the housekeeper had also been baking, filling the larder with cakes and tarts.

Everything we ate in the country was so different. I had never tasted vegetables like this before, and I've never tasted them since. I can remember the sweet-sharp snap of freshly picked Cox's apples even now: the raw green flavour of the runner beans; the musty, earthy smell of the parsnips we stored in sand in the shed. Flavours so deep and intense, they stay with you for ever.

By the time I was fifteen my father was

happier than I had ever seen him. He had started playing tennis, while I wrote short stories and spent hour after hour with my homework, gazing out over the Malverns and the yellow leaves of the damson trees. By sixteen I had started a weekend job preparing vegetables at the local hotel for their magnificent roast Sunday lunches.

My father married the housekeeper and hugged me with tears in his eyes when I showed him the wedding cake with its intricate trellis of icing that I had copied from a book. He died shortly afterwards, playing tennis, and I caught the first train to Birmingham.

IMOGEN STUBBS

So many people these days blame their childhood for ruining their life. I think someone needs to speak up for childhood. I couldn't have been better set up in life – in spite of my father dying when I was thirteen.

We lived in west London on an old wooden boat until then. It seemed spectacular to me and I loved it, but looking back it was daring of my mother to live in a rickety old boat you could only get into down a ladder, with two little children, a dog and a cat. It cost only £600 because a previous inhabitant had shot the postman or something. Now it would be condemned by the social services. We had endless problems with holes, rats and silver fish. The bilge pumps were going the whole time. Lots of people wouldn't let their children stay with us. Finally the boat tangled with an old rusty motorbike, and that was the beginning of the end.

My grandmother lived in Northumberland in a wonderful house on the moors between Rothbury and Scot's Gap, which my step-grandfather had rented so she could be near her family. My mother took us up there often in the holidays. Above, on the hills, were what I thought were two Roman castles. It's rather absurd when I look back. It was so obvious they were follies, but to me they were real.

We had an old Volkswagen mini-bus in which we would drive up, making ourselves car-sick by reading and playing cards in the back. In those days it took forever to get there. One year we got as far as Yorkshire, and then we realised we'd left Simla our Tibetan lion dog behind and we had to go all the way back.

My grandmother was brilliant at understanding what a child really wanted. Her house smelt of polish, not because it was obsessively well kept up, but because there was a corridor that was polished so we could all run and slide on it. One Christmas she built me a go-cart painted yellow, blue and red; another year she found a small paraffin stove on which I could cook hot chocolate. Another present was a sweet shop with little bottles full of real sweets.

She also had a Marie Antoinette kind of farm. We would get up very early in the morning, and Peggy, a land girl in the war who had stayed on, would tell us stories about my mother and my aunt, while she milked the two cows, Bonny and Shirley. She had a separating room where she made the butter and cream. We would stick with her a lot, and feel like her adopted family – she was part of ours.

We collected the eggs from the hens and fed the ducks, then we would eat a huge breakfast (we always had cornflakes with cream and sugar, no milk) and we would be off. We wandered for miles and miles, finding things, making camps, playing kick-the-can, and slithering through tunnels in the bracken – until I heard there might be snakes.

The woods around the lake were laced with streams and stuffed with rhododendrons. In the summer we would make little caves in them. The man who used to look after the grounds chopped up logs so we had seats and tables and we would go and get food from Peggy. I found it exciting to eat sorrel, and blueberries and myrtle that you could get free from nature.

In the summer my step-grandfather enclosed a shallow bit of the lake with a net so that we could swim without going out of our depth. There were trees stretching out over the water and we'd climb along a branch and just jump in. We all had very liberal parents who thought we were quite responsible, but it was probably the older cousins who kept an eye on us. Someone who stopped on the road once had a lion cub in the back of their car, and they let me hold it. I remember thinking it was just part of the extraordinariness of being there.

My life up there was an Enid Blyton, *Swallows and Amazons* cliché of a Sunday serial. My grandmother was the personality behind it all. She was a Katharine Hepburn-ish kind of a person, a successful playwright, very sociable. She gave huge parties for all ages, where everyone sang the songs she wrote.

She died when I was eleven, my step-grandfather remarried and it wasn't our home any more. I drove past recently and it is still beautiful, but there are no children. It was a paradise for children.

EMMA TENNANT

I spent my childhood at Glen, a gothic extravaganza built by my great-grandfather in the middle of the last century, when all he had to do to augment his fortune was toss his gold pince-nez on to a map of the world, peer down at the lucky spot, and then announce that the next thing would be the gold mines at Mysore.

By the time I came to live there this valley with its Loire-type chateau in the county of Peeblesshire was sealed off by the exigencies of war. If the place seemed more open than usual to rabbits, straying sheep and roe deer, it was because the wrought-iron gates into the park and garden had been requisitioned for munitions. But those who lived in the small village clustered round the farm – and those who lived in the Big House, too – were virtually prohibited from leaving the place because of petrol rationing; neighbours who might have been persuaded to pool resources lived simply too far away.

Not that a sense of isolation was anything new in this part of the world. The imagination works full out when confronted by empty hills and miles of untended silver birch forest, which in those days surrounded the valley. James Hogg, the Ettrick Shepherd, wrote many tales of metamorphosis and magic about the denizens of the beautifully named Fethan Wood (on to which my bedroom window looked once it was deemed safe to move upstairs from the basement). Sir Walter Scott and Wordsworth walked to the Gordon Arms in the heart of Yarrow to meet Hogg, the autodidact who in turn walked thirty miles over the hills from his low-windowed shepherd's house to meet them. Such energy and adventurousness made our trips to Innerleithen, five miles away, seem pathetically dull.

Christmas was hardly celebrated there at all. While news of English cousins or friends enjoying days of uninterrupted festivities came up from south of the border, we found the little post office at the top of the brae firmly open on Christmas Day, and the postman delivering mail. Our tree, in the pillared hall hung with Scottish and English portraits, had candles and carefully pre-served pre-war decorations. Once all the candles were lit, villagers came to look at the tree gleaming in the soot-black afternoons of a northern December. But they did no decorating or tinselling themselves. The big shut-down, the Hogmanay saturnalia, still gripped – still continues to grip – a land that, after centuries of Calvinism and puritanism, refuses to relinquish a pagan core.

Of course, Hogmanay was what I looked forward to, too. This was when it was possible to enter a grown-up world – to see, because barriers were down and drink flowed and accordions wheezed – how people really were. After the long meals in the glacial dining room (even colder there than the drawing room with its log fire and great pools of freezing air), I would slip away from the polished table, leaving the relatives who appeared at each meal like weathermen, popping out of their arctic rooms to find sustenance in hot food and drink.

It was exciting – even dangerous – to run down the dark stone stairs to the basement and prepare for a night of First Footing in houses unrecognisable because they had never been seen at night, dressed up to receive the dark stranger. There would be apples, whisky, a coke fire burning high despite rationing. Dancing, thumping on linoleum floors, burling round and round until giddy and scarlet-cheeked, presents and chocolates to mark the death of the old year and the drunken, reeling birth of the new.

January days were quiet and white after the volcanic explosion of Hogmanay. Sometimes I was taken out shooting, standing with chilblained feet for hours in a wood by a pond. There were no organised shoots, because of the war. I suppose there must have been a lot of game about but what we seemed to eat day in day out was rabbit.

Mrs Mackay, the cook, had perfected the art of cooking rabbit – in a tomato and carrot sauce, as a Wiener schnitzel. She grilled it with mustard and each time we duly pretended to be taken in and to have thought the dish to be something quite unobtainable in the war. It was indeed delicious and after a breakfast of dried egg, which was kept in a hot cupboard in the pantry and often resembled something fossilised and long forgotten, the triumph of the rabbit was all the more welcome. Whether the relatives who came to stay thought so is quite another matter.

It is only since writing *Pemberley,* my sequel to *Pride and Prejudice,* that I have come to see the similarities between the world Jane Austen described and my own childhood. For one thing, aunts, uncles and grandparents visited Glen for what seemed an interminable time. There would be a Lady Catherine de Burgh figure, determined to maintain standards as she had known them in a gilded Edwardian youth, when baths were drawn for the ladies and clothes ironed and laid out before dinner. For that dinner to consist of just one course would have been completely out of the question. And then for that one course to be rabbit! As well as the wicked Lady Catherine type, there were sycophants and *malades imaginaires* and plain bores: it is hard to imagine how my mother could have put up with them all, meal after meal and day after day, especially in the depths of winter.

It was not her place to escape as I did as a child on New Year's Eve to the lower regions of that strange, castellated house, but I could pass unseen, run down to the kitchen, prepare for the excitement of the First Footers, or just help Mrs Mackay with her latest rabbit disguise.

COLIN THUBRON

The first six years of my life left me with just a handful of joggled memories: my father was a professional soldier in Italy and North Africa during the war, and my mother, sister, nanny and I moved from pillar to post mostly around the south of England. Nowhere seemed very like a permanent home. I never questioned my father's absence, but when he was due to return, in early 1946, I realised I couldn't remember him.

I went to the railway station hanging on to my mother's hand, wondering what he was going to look like. Crowds of servicemen were coming down the platform and I scanned every face: little fat men, thin men, gawky men. Suddenly, a staff stick was thrown out of a train window, and my mother said, 'That'll be him.' He'd always had a great sense of humour. Out came this tall, handsome man covered in medals – he was every boy's dream of a father and he was mine. I was thrilled by his height and military splendour.

When the war ended we bought Pheasants Hatch, near Uckfield, and for me it was a kind of paradise. I was suddenly let out into what seemed to be an enormous garden, with that rather lovely Sissinghurst style of rooms and avenues and little bosky passages. I felt released, not only from wartime strictures, but into a literal garden of Eden.

Although we lived in the countryside I wasn't a typical country boy. The farming year was part of my landscape but I wasn't really involved. Life at Pheasants Hatch created its own world – a garden that my mother loved and extended year after year. I was a sensitive child and relished the safety.

(Possibly because of this security, I have rarely felt in danger even on my travels.) I wrote dreadful poetry in the garden for years; every butterfly that flew over the hedge received a eulogy.

Looking back at my childhood, there seem to be no ripples on the pond, or they were so unimportant that I have forgotten them. I was a dreamy child, fairly self-sufficient, creating characters and dramas around me. (My mother remembers when she came to pick me up at parties there would always be one little boy playing by himself in the corner, and it would be me.) I was happy with my sister Carol and a favourite army of tin soldiers, or walking in the woods with my whippet, Vali. As a terrible romantic, I fell in love with a little gypsy-looking girl with whom I went to school. I invited her to my birthday party and she gave me a cut-out book. But she had already cut out all the bits herself: I still remember my disappointment to this day, and I went off her right away.

At seven, I was cast out of paradise when I was sent to school. I hated the separation from my family and from Pheasants Hatch, although of course it was the best education

201

for me. But it was suddenly very isolated: there is nothing so total in later life, and the pain of those partings was awful. My father had become military attaché in Canada, so for three years I went back and forth across the Atlantic to school. Sometimes you would say goodbye and get in the plane, which would taxi down the runway and then not take off because of fog or engine trouble. Back you came into the departure lounge where your parents were waiting, and you would have these 'stolen hours' as we called them: wonderful in a way, but still rather desperate. But I loved my prep school, and in a day or two – in the callous way of children – my homesickness would be gone.

My fascination with travelling probably started then. I flew to Canada in a rather dashing four-engine Stratocruiser. In those days, you might stop in Prestwick, Reykjavik, Newfoundland, Labrador. I was intrigued to be in these different places. We lived another kind of country life those summers on the vast Gatineau River near Ottawa: fishing, swimming and generally running wild.

After we returned to Pheasants Hatch, I went to Eton. In many ways I was living in a kind of dream through much of public school. However, Eton was kind to eccentrics, and on the whole I was happy. But it was still the garden at home, where the gold and silver ornamental pheasants wandered, that pulled me. (The garden is just as important where I live now, in London. When I first viewed the house, I ran outside, looked at the garden and said, 'I'll buy it!' When people asked whether the house had central heating, I didn't know.)

It's odd how cloudless the years at Pheasants Hatch seem. Retrospectively, I realise that compared with later life and the lives of most other children, it was marvellously happy. My sister was fundamental to my childhood: often we had just one another in that enclosed paradise. She was more practical and energetic than I was and did everything terribly well, while I tagged along dreamily behind. When I was nineteen, on the verge of taking up my first job, she was killed in a skiing accident. Her death seemed to come down like a guillotine between one part of my life and the other. My adult life began when she died.

ROSE TREMAIN

'Ties with the earth and farm animals and growing things are never made at all unless they are made early,' says the American writer, Willa Carther in her short story *Neighbour Rosicky*. In the same way, I think, close bonds are formed between individuals and big cities. Those who spend their childhoods in London, Paris or New York perceive themselves to be true citizens of those places in a way that no latecomer ever can.

I grew up in post-war London. We had a terraced house in Chelsea with no garden. Ten houses along, there was a bomb site. The walk to school, past the bomb site, took twenty minutes. On 'smog' days, my sister and I were told to tie hankies round our noses and mouths, and by the time we got to school, the hankies would be grey. London then – even Chelsea, which has always had pretensions to smartness – was a poor, dirty city.

When asked about my childhood, however, it is scarcely ever about London that I find myself talking. It's about my grandfather's farm in Hampshire.

It was called Linkenholt. Every holiday, a car would be sent for us, and at the end of a long journey that meandered through Virginia Water, Bagshot and Winchfield, my sister and I would find ourselves in a big airy room that smelled of beeswax polish and dusty chintz, looking out over a sloping lawn, a rose garden and a spinney of larch and ash and chestnut.

Reclaiming this room, holiday by holiday, was both the most exquisite and the saddest pleasure of my first eleven years. It was ours and yet not ours. We would inhabit it for weeks at a time, and then the car would return us to London. We loved it absolutely and at the same time knew the folly of loving it too much. What it held, of course, on those first evenings, was the already felt presence of the next day. In the silence, or not-quite-silence of the Hampshire night, we would remember what waking up was going to be like: the chintz would be drawn back; instead of our grey skirts and Aertex blouses, we would put on green dungarees and striped T-shirts, known in those days as 'cotton jumpers'. 'We're here,' my sister would announce, 'we're at Linkenholt.'

Four years older than me, my sister Joanna was at that time convinced that real life was made more vivid if you ceased to be a girl and turned yourself into a film star for most of your waking life. All through our years at Linkenholt, my sister pretended to be Deborah Kerr. She had seen *King Solomon's Mines* seven times. She knew hundreds of lines by heart. But to be Deborah Kerr, she needed someone – and the only someone she had was me – to play all the supporting roles. So it was mainly as Stewart Granger (with lines like 'chin up, darling. We'll make it across this infernal desert yet!') that I lived my tantalisingly happy 'country childhood'. The make-believe was apt. This was not our home but we pretended it was. And we believed that here, we could become whatever we chose.

One of the things we chose to become were riders. There were no docile ponies waiting for us in a paddock, but Daubeny, the fox-faced man who cared for the hens, had an old carthorse that he drove round the rows of hen houses, and we persuaded him to let us take it in turns to ride the horse while he drove the cart, in return for helping to collect the eggs and scatter the feed. Whole days were spent with Daubeny. If he tired of us, he never complained. At sundown, in summer, we'd still be there, jogging back to the farmyard with him, Joanna's D K auburn plait still clipped to her hair with kirby grips, but my paltry Stewart Granger too tired, too happy to be convincing any more.

The weather, at Linkenholt, always seemed obedient to the seasons: snow on Christmas Eve, as we were taken in the car past sighing white forests to a party where the tree was lit with real candles. Snow on Christmas morning, thick and flat and unmarked except by the tiny stencillings of birds' feet. Then in spring, a cold petulant breeze, followed by a sudden warm lull and a bright glitter on the yards of daffodils. Even the summers were warm. My mother sat by the rose garden in a cane chair, wearing white-rimmed sunglasses. In the orchard, my grandmother, lame by this time and mourning the loss of her two sons till her death, would take us to see her favourite tree, a greengage. The skin of the fruit she handed down was hot from the sun.

The only season we never saw at Linkenholt was the autumn. I can imagine how it might have looked to us, had we ridden our bikes or Daubeny's horse down the farm lanes in October. My thoughts would have turned, probably, to a conker harvest abundant beyond imagining, and Joanna, surely, would have seen in the reddening copper beeches the exact, the perfect colour replica of Deborah Kerr's hair.

Most cities, including London, are to me at their most agreeable in autumn, the harsh edges of them softened a little by light and leaf fall. In London, on a fine autumn day, I know without question that I belong there. Yet I don't live there now, nor in the heart of the country either, but on the edge of a city (from our garden, you can't see the city, but it's there, just beyond the wall). It's as if, pulled equally in childhood by town and field, I've settled, in the middle of my life, for neither, waiting for some future day when I will finally make up my mind.

WILLIAM TREVOR

I didn't have a country childhood, but the country was always at the end of the street and the street was never long. I grew up in what John Betjeman called 'the small towns of Ireland' – in my case, Mitchelstown, squat between the towering Galtee mountains and the Knockmealdowns, Youghal by the sea, Skibbereen lost somewhere in the back of beyond. There was Tipperary as well, and hilly Enniscorthy, and Portaloise in the great flatness of the midland plain. Galway, where my childhood ended, is a city: grey majestic City of the Tribes, with Connemara on its doorstep.

Turf smoke, often an ingredient in Irish country air, smells different in a town: I know I'm home when, yet again, I'm reminded of that. I know I'm home when I see the weary heads of cabbage and the drooping green ferns of the carrot bunches outside the vegetable shops of my provincial childhood. The small towns I'm still drawn back to, and always will be, are higgledy-piggledy, thrown together, modest in all things: the richer world of the country tolerates them, its natural charm reminding their ugly-duckling presence that it is there on sufferance. One day, perhaps, there'll be a swan to answer back, but so far there's no sign of that.

Every summer when we lived in Youghal – in the mid-Thirties – we left the town and spent four or five weeks in a remote bay along the Waterford coast, my father making the daily journey to the bank where he worked by bicycle. My mother borrowed tents, including a marquee, from a man who'd bought them in error at an auction, and these were erected in front of a ruined one-storey Georgian house on a cliff. She also borrowed a lorry, into which were loaded chests-of-drawers, dressing-tables, beds, chairs, an oil stove with an oven, the kitchen table, and other household items, including our new Philips wireless set and a wind-up gramophone.

Camping wasn't all that common in Co. Waterford in those days, and had a pioneering feel to it. Milk had to be fetched from a distant farmhouse, water from a spring in the glen, baskets of peas and potatoes from Ballyquin, half an hour's walk along the strand. Woods stretched for miles behind the derelict house and somewhere in the middle of them lived a man with rheumy eyes called Paddy Lyndon, who used to bring us mushrooms in a knotted red handkerchief: try as we would – my brother, my sister and myself – we could never find his cottage. But nearer the house itself, in a tumbled-down outbuilding, we discovered an old motorcar with brass headlamps – one of the first, Paddy Lyndon told us, that had taken to the roads in Ireland.

Glencairn House the place was called, owned by an Englishman who had left during the Troubles and now rarely returned. 'A right gentleman,' Paddy Lyndon stated and my father, who had to write to him in order to get permission for our camping, agreed that this must be so. We peered through the cracks of the boarded windows but could distinguish nothing in the darkness that kept the rooms' secrets: we never knew if there was furniture there or not. In the hedge that ran along the short avenue to the house I was shown eggs in a thrush's nest.

My father set snares every night. I was standing beside Henry Reilly the time he shot a rabbit. Known locally as the laziest man in Ireland, Henry Reilly in my own view was also the nicest. Red-haired and bulky, an Irish country bachelor not unlike many of those who wander in and out of my fiction, he was the son of the farmhouse that supplied the milk.

Sometimes he took me with him on the cart to the creamery and on the way back we would stop at a crossroads half-and-half – a shop that is a grocery as well as a public house. He had a bottle of stout himself, and bought me lemonade and biscuits. He would settle himself down with his elbows on the counter, exchanging whatever news there was while the woman who'd served us weighed sugar into coarse black paper-bags. Most of the day it took, going to the creamery with Henry Reilly.

I weeded a field of marigolds with him, a task that didn't require much energy because we stopped whenever he began a new story and he had a lot of stories: about his ancestors, and '98, and the Troubles, the Black and Tans, the time Michael Collins passed near by. At 12 o'clock we went back to the farmhouse and sat down in the kitchen to a meal of potatoes, which were tumbled out on to a newspaper in the centre of the table. Mrs Reilly, all in black, was there, and her brother, whom none of us ever saw without his hat, her daughter Biddy, and an old man – said to be Mrs Reilly's uncle – known as 'Blood-and–'ouns!' because he so often employed the expression. The old man left the farm only once a year, to walk to Ardmore and get drunk on the day before Corpus Christi.

I remember that stillness of the woods, and the sun burning my arms in the marigold field, and clambering down the clay of the cliffs to the sea – in which I once made a nuisance of myself by nearly drowning. No one else ever appeared on the mile of pale strand that began with shingle at the bottom of the cliffs, became soft sand, then hard. Horseflies bothered us when we lay on the grass in front of the derelict house, the wireless turned on when it was time for Henry Hall. One day I put my foot into my boot and was stung by a wasp.

I went back not long ago. From Ardmore or Ballyquin you can see the derelict house, towards which the cliff edge has relentlessly advanced over the years. Gaunt and white, the Reilly's farmhouse – yellow-washed in my time – is more wisely positioned, still acres away from that crumbling cliff. A lone woman, with buckets hanging from the handlebars of a bicycle, searches for shellfish on the rocks. Barley grows in the marigold field. The short-cuts of those summers have gone, but the midges still come with the gloom of evening.

For me, all of it has remained a yardstick for country matters. The easy-going household of the farm is what I turn to first when I think of country people. The fallen roof of the house, the boarded windows, the grassy yard, the tumbled-down outbuilding where the brass-lamped car was: all this is how ruins should be. There is nothing spectacular about the landscape, yet it is the landscape with which I instinctively compare all others. 'Why on earth don't you buy that house?' people say to me. But that of course would spoil things.

JOANNA TROLLOPE

I was born in circumstances which are hardly permitted nowadays – in a bedroom in a Cotswold rectory, attended by the village doctor (no doubt in a three-piece tweed suit) and my grandmother's oversized dachshund. It was December 1943 and I imagine everyone was cold, hungry and war-weary except me. My father, serving with the army in India, knew nothing about it for ages.

It was, perhaps, a bizarre arrival but it gave me a sense of place. I can still drive down Minchinhampton's steep street into the market square and look up at the window behind which I gave my first yell – a privilege denied my hospital-born daughters and their contemporaries. This sense of place meant that although my childhood was largely spent in York, then Stourbridge in Worcestershire and Reigate in Surrey, I have a persistent conviction that it was *actually* spent in Gloucestershire, in my grandparents' house, where we went for holidays.

My grandfather was Rector of Minchinhampton, a big village, even in the Forties and Fifties. He had been a Bush Brother in Australia before the First World War (the Bishop of Queensland had advertised for young priests who could 'pray like angels and ride like cowboys') and subsequently never used a car when a horse would do. Opposite the Rectory across the street were the stables, which smelt of horse and hay and leather, and were as horsey as I ever wished to get. I was given riding lessons with Mr Reginald Bryce at Hyde and was green with panicky nausea before and during every one.

Minchinhampton was a self-sufficient place, even then. Round the wide market place and the main street was a baker (hot rolls on Sunday mornings), a butcher with a sawdusted floor, a chemist with bottles of coloured liquid in the windows, a post office and two drapers, Top Og's and Bottom Og's, which sold as many things to mend clothes with as clothes. The church, with its much-admired spire, had a proper black-garbed toothless verger and was redolent of incense – my grandfather was pretty High Church. But the glory of the place, then as much as today, was its common.

High, wide and open, its sheep-nibbled surface indented with ancient bumps and barrows, the common ran for several miles north, west and south until it fell off the edges and down into the Stroud and Nailsworth valleys. We walked on it every day, in all weathers, at a terrific pace set by my grandmother and surrounded by a skittering pack of dachshunds. Sometimes we walked as far as Stroud – four and a half miles – with a return journey up the Butter Row, which felt like climbing the side of a house. A day without a walk was not to be contemplated.

Nor was a day without dressing up. In the Rectory's attics, immense ball-dress trunks held shepherdess costumes, Turkish slippers, First World War tin hats and obsolete firearms. The attic was the place to put these things on but the garden was the place to parade them. As the common was to Minchinhampton, so the garden was to the Rectory – a wonderful place of sloping lawns and broad grass terraces and trees hidden behind a gaunt Victorian house. Around the huge garden my brother Andrew and I marched for hours, in clanking swords and trailing trains and greatcoats, to an audience of nobody, perfectly satisfied.

Yet for all these convivial pleasures, the thing I remember with most gratitude was being able to do things alone. It was perfectly safe to, then, and we took it for granted – roaming around the village and the common, spending ages staring at lichens or puddles or snail shells, or wedged in a yew tree in the rain wondering exactly *how* poisonous the berries would be to eat. I retain an impression of freedom and simultaneous security, as if that airy Cotswold upland belonged to me in a perfectly natural way. And, driving across it now almost half a century later, I don't feel much different: I may know it doesn't really belong to me – but I also know it once did.

MARK TULLY

I suppose what I remember most about my childhood is a series of tearful farewells: of departures from very happy homes for various boarding schools.

It all began when I was about five, when I started at the New School in Darjeeling. My memory is not very exact, but I do recall driving from our home in Regent's Park, Calcutta to Sealdah railway station in the centre of the city, tears streaming down my face as I thought of morning rides through the lush green Bengal countryside; family breakfasts at the swimming club and teas at Tolly, as the Tollygunge Club was always known, after my parents had finished their round of golf. I also thought of the kindly servants I was leaving behind and even of our strict nanny. The crying lasted until well after the Darjeeling Mail left Sealdar.

By the next morning, when we reached Siliguri at the foot of the Himalayas, I had recovered. There the tiny train that was to zigzag and loop its way slowly up the mountainside to Darjeeling stood waiting for us. I proudly told my fellow passengers that my father was a director of the Darjeeling Himalayan Railway. It was one of the many companies managed by the firm of which he was a partner. Eventually the gallant little engine made it to the highest point, Ghum, let off a great cloud of steam, and relaxed as it freewheeled down to Darjeeling. We walked from the station up to the New School. I had been given a stamped postcard to send home, which I handed to the housemistress, with just the words 'Have come safely and was not sick' written on it.

In fact, the New School saved me from a far worse fate. If it hadn't been for the Second World War and the New School, I would probably have started my boarding-school career at a pre-preparatory school in England and there wouldn't ever have been holidays in Calcutta.

The school was established during the war to educate the children of the Calcutta business community who could not go back to Britain because there were no boats. It closed as soon as the P&O resumed some semblance of a service. There were boys and girls ranging from four to eighteen.

Darjeeling was then a small hill station surrounded by tea gardens and dominated by the mighty Kanchenjunga, still to me the most majestic of the Himalayas. Considering how young many of us there were, we had remarkable freedom. Whenever I smell the fresh scent of pine trees I am reminded of the forest above our school. We used to walk through it to get to the camp where American soldiers gave us chocolates. I had my first cigarette in that forest, too. I still remember the brand: Scissors. The other smell that always reminds me of Darjeeling is the scent of drying leaves in a tea-garden factory. We spent short holidays from the New School at one of the Darjeeling tea gardens managed by my father's firm. To this day I drink that champagne of teas.

In early 1945, before the war had ended, my father managed to get us berths on a ship to Britain. He stayed on in Calcutta, leaving my mother to cope with six children (my youngest sister was then less than one year old); my grandfather, who had no desire to leave Calcutta; and Nanny, who was not exactly over the moon at returning to a land where there would be no servants to do all the hard work. Somehow mother got us to Winchester, where we moved from rented house to rented house until my father left India and got a job in Manchester.

The house I remember best was Pilgrims, set on the top of Compton Downs, in Berkshire. But unfortunately most of my time there was spent behind the high walls of nearby Twyford School. Each term was preceded by the inevitable tearful farewell. It was a complete contrast to the free-and-easy New School. We were let out only once a week to walk under strict supervision over the Twyford Downs – not the best way to enjoy that beautiful countryside, now sadly defiled.

Next I moved to Marlborough College, set in starker, bleaker countryside. I did have more freedom than at Twyford as we were allowed to cycle, but being innately lazy I did not often get beyond Savernake Forest, where I was able to renew my love affair with tobacco.

By this time my home was the Old Vicarage, in a village in Cheshire. On some signposts it still boasted of being Peover Superior, although the postal address was the more modest Over, as against Lower, Peover. Ours was a spacious house with a long tarmac drive, sometimes mistaken by picnickers for a country lane until my father put them right in no uncertain terms. Summer holidays were marred by my mother's insistence that I play cricket with the sons of Cheshire's gentry. I loathed the game and wasn't over fond of most of the cricketers. All I wanted to do was stay at home because I loved the garden, the orchard, the ponies, the pigs, and of course the large self-contained Tully family. That's why, I suppose, I still had at least a little weep when I left for my last term at Marlborough.

I have not lost the habit of weeping, because even now I often break down when leaving those I love. That's the legacy of my childhood, much of it spent in beautiful countryside that I couldn't enjoy.

MARCO PIERRE WHITE

I was born in Leeds in December 1961, but for much of my early life I lived in Italy with my mother in the town of Badorino near Lake Garda. We lived in a house called Molino – the mill – and my days were spent by the riverbank. Right from the beginning, I felt a connection with nature: one of my earliest and fondest memories is of playing hide-and-seek sitting in the fruit trees, munching cherries as we waited to be found. The hillside behind Molino was terraced and planted with vines, which we sat beneath to eat the incredibly sweet grapes. These images are very vivid in my mind. I don't have such clear memories of speech, perhaps because my mother always spoke to me in Italian, my father in English.

My big brothers Graham and Clive (my mother must have got her own way when I was named) did some work for a man called Signor Lorenzo who lived on the other side of the river. He used to pay them in baskets of peaches, which he would winch across the river on a rope.

My brothers took me fishing and when they'd hooked a fish, they'd let me hold the rod and wind it in. Soon, I started to catch fish every day and put them, still alive, in a bucket of water. Each night I'd take the bucket home and put it on the ledge by the front door. Every morning I'd come down, the fish would be gone, and I'd be absolutely furious. My mother used to tell me the birds had eaten them. But in reality, when I went to bed she would walk back to the river and let the fish go. She knew I'd forgive the birds.

Graham, Clive and I spent hours on the river; we'd hollow out bamboo shoots and use them as snorkels, or pass afternoons catching water snakes. Friends nearby had great galvanised tanks and they would lift off the top to show us the wriggling eels caught in the river at night.

It was interesting being brought up in two cultures, one very Latin, one working-class British. But when I was six my mother died, so my days in Italy disappeared. Did I miss being there? When you're a child, you do not question, you just accept. Because of my mother's death, I felt that some far greater injustice had been done to me: leaving Italy behind was irrelevant. Once, much later in England, walking along a riverbank, I smelt a certain scent that reminded me very strongly of my mother. A few years afterwards, a girl made me a cup of camomile tea and I recognised the smell. I must have walked on some camomile by the river and it brought back the memory of my mother drinking that tea.

In Leeds, I was fortunate because I lived on the outskirts of the city in a district called Moortown. At the top of my road was a golf course; I'd walk across this into the Earl of Harewood's estate and see grey partridge, woodcock, hares: I suppose it was my playground. Many days were spent birdnesting, generally alone, as my brothers were a lot older. I idolised my brother Graham. Probably the last thing a thirteen-year-old boy wants is his six-year-old brother hanging around, but because our mother had died, he had a duty towards me, and fulfilled it fantastically. Graham had an amazing knowledge of wood- or field-craft, call it what you will. I've seen him call hares with a sucking noise he makes on the side of his hand. When they are out of range to be shot, he'll make this sound and they'll come. Even to this day, he is still the best shot and one of the most natural fishermen I've met.

I can remember catching my first brown trout a mile from my house. I was brought up by the River Wharfe which I think has some of the largest shoals of grayling in Britain. We used centre pin reels; we would trot for them down the rapids and catch thirty or forty grayling in a day. Grayling is the best eating fish in the river and it's good-looking, too. I also like dry-fly fishing for chub and dace, but my favourite to catch is barbel, the strongest fighting fish in the river.

As a young boy, my ambition was to be a gamekeeper. I recall the head forester on the Harewood Estate, Bert Meredith. Once he was taking me and a friend along a bridle path in his Land-Rover when he suddenly stopped. A female woodcock walked across the path with her young, and Bert said: 'That's one of the rarest sights in nature, and you'll be lucky if you ever see it again.' And I never have.

NIGEL WILLIAMS

I was born and brought up in London's suburbs and the country first became a possibility for me when I stood waiting with my brother and my mother by the bus stop near our house for the all-night coach to the Lake District.

In those days the coach took about ten hours. There were weird, grimly-lit filling stations, there were empty arterial roads and, in the early morning, after a few hours awkward sleep, you would be jolted awake by switchback rising and falling, violent turns around hairpin bends, and the growl of the gears as the coach climbed and climbed...

The Lake District had mountains. My mother's friend Mabel – who was from Newcastle, wore a beret, carried a walking stick and, for reasons that were never satisfactorily explained, was always referred to as Auntie – used to say 'Remember dear! These mountains can kill you!' From my first sight of them from the coach, they scared and excited me. Later, I would look up at them from the comfort of my room in the Skiddaw Hotel and wait for them to slither round the side of the lake and clomp towards me across the bracken, intent on my destruction. And later still – always after Auntie Mabel had walked us up to a small bump at the edge of Derwentwater called Castle Crag 'to get our legs going' – I would join my mother, my brother and my courtesy aunt and trek out towards Great Gable, Helvellyn or Scafell Pike.

I never really came to terms with any other mountains. I occasionally glimpsed images of large white ones with ski slopes, pointed bits and wooden chalets all over them on biscuit tins. Once we drove through Scotland but Scottish mountains, in my view, all looked and sounded the same and seemed to go on too long. The Welsh mountains were impossible to pronounce and had a disapproving air. The mountains of the English Lake District – looking as they did like some giant's relief map – were, to me, the essence of what the countryside should mean to a child. They were escape and yet they felt like home; dangerous – so Auntie Mabel kept saying – yet small enough to conquer.

Our holidays were always carefully structured. After Castle Crag came Catbells, a beautiful green hill of around 1,000 feet on the other side of Derwentwater from Keswick. After Catbells there was Causey Pike, an elegant and faintly sinister peak culminating in something that always reminded me of a giant wart, and then there was Helvellyn and Scafell Pike. Once we went without Auntie Mabel up a mountain my mother said was Dollywagon Pike, but turned out to be something completely different. I remember standing in the middle of a sea of dark, tough grass, looking at a row of unfamiliar peaks while my brother howled accusingly at my mother:

'You're lost! Admit it! You're lost!'

In the second week, for two days we rested. I went fishing in a beck up by Dockray above Ullswater and once took out an eight-inch trout that the hotel cooked for my tea. My brother and I went rowing on Derwentwater. And then, on the last three or four days, Auntie Mabel would take us 'somewhere special!' We would pack sandwiches, take a bus out of town and toil up a hill, marked by huge, threatening stones, past rivers and beyond tarns to an unfamiliar peak where Mabel would begin an elaborate geography lesson. Year after year I used to imagine I was getting closer to knowing all the mountains and their names, but I never did. Then one year it was announced that Mabel wouldn't be going with us. She's dead now but I can still remember her Newcastle accent, her industrial-strength stockings and her sensible school-teacher's shoes.

Indeed, when I look back now and try to understand why my idea of the countryside still lies north of Kendal and south of Carlisle, I suspect that it wasn't really a matter of landscape. The Lakes were full of such highly entertaining people. There were hikers in anoraks, woolly hats and large boots who came from places I had never seen, such as Sheffield and Bradford. They were very concerned to greet you as you toiled up the narrow paths, fringing the becks and gills, where white water spilled down off the mountain, and when you got back to the hotel in the evening, they seemed amazingly impressed that you had managed to get up Old Man's Bottom or The Crack of Doom or whatever chunk of pre-Cambrian rock it had been decreed you should climb that day.

There were the shepherds, often dressed with a curious formality, puffing on cigarettes or whistling to their dogs outside the farm that still lies on the road from Seathwaite to Scafell Pike and Gable. There were the other families who sat with us at dinner, faces raw and red from the mountains, and there was my family, who were not as they were in London. They were nicer and wiser. There was my mother massaging her aching feet, my brother solemnly ticking off species in his *Observer Book of Birds* and dear Auntie Mabel, feet braced against the angry mountain, beret well back on her head, all her energies focused on giving a London kid a country childhood he's never forgotten.

GOOGIE WITHERS

I was seven when I first saw the English countryside. It was cool, green and exciting. If I had been old enough to use such a word, I might have described it as exotic. India, where I was born and had lived until then, was to me the normal, the everyday. My father, a naval officer, told me that I was conceived in the Garden of Eden and that, even before I was born, I'd had adventures. During the First World War, he was based in the Middle East. When my mother was six months pregnant with me the situation was so dangerous that she had to be evacuated. She rode into the desert and camped for two days before sailing across the Red and Arabian seas to Karachi, where I was born.

As my father was part of the Raj and a sahib, we had a large house in Chittagong and numerous servants. I remember one ayah who loved me. My real name is Georgette Lizette, but she called me Googie, which is Hindi for little pigeon or dove, and I've been called that ever since.

Another ayah, called Josephine, was a beast incarnate. I was lively by temperament and restless at night because of the splints I was made to wear to straighten my legs. Josephine slept on the floor by my bed and her blazing eyes would glare at me through the parted mosquito net if I disturbed her. She would hit my head hard with her knuckles, saying that, if I told my mother, she would poison both of us. I was so terrified that it wasn't until we were on our way to England, having left Josephine behind, that I told my mother everything. She was devastated.

But there were good times. I loved the evenings when my parents went to the British club and returned late. Josephine found it dull sitting in my room so she would take me down to the servants' quarters, where everyone chatted in Hindi. Then there were the dancing lessons. A doctor suggested that, rather than wear splints, I should learn to dance. This straightened my legs and was the start of my career.

I remember escaping from the summer heat of Chittagong and going up to Assam by train. My father had his own carriage with bathrooms and bedrooms, which were panelled in a richly polished dark wood, and upholstered in deeply buttoned velvet. A steam engine pulled us panting and whistling around precipitous bends as we made our way slowly up to the hills. I remember the vivid colours of saris as women walked gracefully in line across the fields, and the sight of huge white bullocks.

My father's brother had a tea plantation in Assam, green hill upon green hill, with a spacious house surrounded by enormous verandas. He had teams of elephants and I was given my own baby elephant. I would spend the day on its back while we followed its mother around as she shifted logs and waded through streams. It was idyllic.

But it was the English countryside that became my real love. I adored it the moment I saw it and have adored it ever since. We went to Dorset where there were castles, hills that stretched for miles, flowers and sea birds. The freedom was incredible. In India, there was no question of going beyond the compound of our house, walking in the streets, or going into the bazaar. We only went out in a car driven by my father's naval driver.

My mother, who had Dutch, French and German blood, and spoke four languages, had wanted to live in Paris but my father's strait-laced sisters thought it would be better if we settled with them in Swanage. My aunts lived in a typical average-sized country house, which at first seemed incredibly small compared with our huge, almost palatial, home in India. And instead of teams of servants there was an old retainer, a maid and a gardener called Lovelace. I was always praising him for the beautiful flowers he grew: we didn't have those exquisite English flowers in India. He would, in all honesty, tell me that the little people had told him exactly where to plant them.

Shortly after we moved to England, I was sent to boarding school in Kent. I didn't have any difficulty adjusting; I just behaved outrageously. I was used to being waited on and was dreadfully spoiled. I was often spanked, but the school was very tolerant, regarding me as quite clever. I wasn't unhappy. Dorset and chalk cliffs and coves and secret walks were always there to return to in the holidays. Fortunately they still are.

SUSANNAH YORK

Four miles inland from the west coast of Scotland, the rambling grey house of my childhood stood high on a hill, buffeted by winds and blessed with exceptional views. When I looked out of my bedroom window, beyond the miles of willow trees, I could see all the way to the islands of Arran and Ailsa Craig.

This was stone-wall country, surrounded by farms, fields and copses full of mushrooms, blackberries and wildflowers. I soon learned not to pick the bluebells because they would die, but I remember spending many hours collecting primroses, king cups and cowslips.

Our garden had a herbaceous border and daffodils, as well as roses along one side of the house, but the wind made it difficult to grow many flowers. Instead, there was a kitchen garden with peas, beans, carrots, strawberries, raspberries and blackcurrants. At the front of the house, there were fields for the ponies. These, together with our ducks, pigs, sheep and dogs, meant animals formed an important part of my childhood.

The property was a sort of smallholding and its old wash house, henhouse and the disused pigsties were transformed into extra little homes where my sisters Carolyn, Mary Jane and I would play.

Whether we were rambling, riding, picnicking, visiting castles or camping out for the night, there was a remarkable freedom in whatever we did. I still don't take well to feeling shut in. There were no barbed wire fences, no dangers in roaming the fields for miles on end. Restraint was unknown, so we climbed over the walls and jumped over gates and simply respected other people's land. Mind you, I remember getting into terrible trouble with one farmer who caught us playing cowboys and Indians in his irresistible long grass, meant for hay, and for sliding down the haystacks.

So many of our games were played outside, even in bleak weather. The one we called Treasure Island was the best. I'd draw a map, then we'd use it to look for the treasure I'd hidden earlier – somehow I'd manage to forget the location so I could join in the search. The game required each person to be a specific character and I always seemed to be the wicked pirate. When it was wet, we'd play in our house's original Victorian chapel, which had been converted into the playroom. We'd perform plays and rollerskate on its wooden floors. And I was curator of my own small museum, for which I charged people a penny entrance fee.

My school was in the coastal town of Troon. Usually I cycled for miles down lonely lanes and main roads to get there but on rainy days, my stepfather would drive me. As soon as we were out of sight of my mother, I'd stand on the running board while he whisked me down the open roads. He'd let me jump off in a hidden spot just round the corner from the school, because I was so embarrassed that we owned a car. Sometimes in winter the weather was too harsh to drive. When I had appendicitis, the snow was so thick that my mother had to trudge for five miles to the nearest hospital with me on a sledge.

After school, I'd rush home to walk my dogs. But when my mother, an avid horse lover, started to teach me to ride, I didn't hurry quite so much. She had three wild Irish ponies and believed the only way to learn to ride was bareback. She also believed that if you fell off, you should get back on immediately. When I was seven or eight, I'd find myself haring round the field after school on a pony named Comet: I fell off half a dozen times a night.

After two or three years, I was given a Highland pony of my own called Morag. I'd ride her bareback down to the coast where we'd gallop along the sand and into the sea. I'd get completely carried away by focusing on one of the islands, magically forgetting what was behind us. Then we'd canter back along the beach to dry off before returning home.

On Sunday mornings – although not every week – we'd go to church. Sometimes it would be to the Presbyterian church where the priest (who looked like God, as depicted by William Blake) would terrify us by hurling damnation over our heads. Or we'd attend the rather milder service at the Protestant church.

Saturday mornings would be spent with my stepfather at Togs Café in Troon, where I would sit by the sea eating ice cream. I love that sea, just as I love the whole area. Although I had little reason to return after my family left in my teenage years, it was many, many years before I stopped considering Scotland my home.

The publishers hope that this book has given you enjoyable reading. Large Print Books are especially designed to be as easy to see and hold as possible. If you wish a complete list of our books please ask at your local library or write directly to:

Magna Large Print Books
Magna House, Long Preston,
Skipton, North Yorkshire.
BD23 4ND

This Large Print Book for the partially sighted, who cannot read normal print, is published under the auspices of

THE ULVERSCROFT FOUNDATION